Charles R. Knight
AUTOBIOGRAPHY OF AN ARTIST

Charles R. Knight

Autobiography
of an Artist

❦

FOREWORD BY
RAY HARRYHAUSEN AND RAY BRADBURY

INTRODUCTION BY WILLIAM STOUT

ILLUSTRATIONS BY MARK SCHULTZ

APPRECIATIONS BY
JOHN FLYNN, JOHN HARRIS, MARK NORELL,
MICHAEL NOVACEK, IAN TATTERSALL,
AND RHODA KNIGHT KALT

EDITED BY JIM OTTAVIANI

G.T. LABS : ANN ARBOR

Book design by Wesley B. Tanner/Passim Editions

ISBN 0-9660106-7-1 (hardcover)
ISBN 0-9660106-8-X (softcover)

Library of Congress Control Number: 2005924222

www.gt-labs.com

Contents

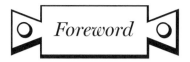

Foreword

Charles R. Knight's dinosaur paintings and drawings have more than just a realistic surface quality about them. Very evident was that added nobility of inspiration and dedication which separates the draughtsman from the true creator.

Knight was not only one of the first to reconstruct prehistoric life in a romantic way but the first to work in close collaboration with paleontologists in trying to achieve scientifically accurate anatomy. He would even resort to the ultimate in dedication by modeling the animal in three dimensional form before attempting to paint it on canvas. His long experience in drawing and painting live modern animals in zoos and his romantic and vivid imagination gave prehistoric reconstructions a charisma only found in living creatures.

The influence of Knight's paintings and reconstructions extended into other fields of endeavor. Most present day illustrators of prehistoric life have his early paintings to thank for their inspiring effect. In the world of motion pictures Willis O'Brien and myself were enormously stimulated by Knight's visions of the world of the past as we created new adventures in the world of fantasy and imagination. O'Brien was the first filmmaker to realize prehistoric animals on film making them the stars of *The Lost World* and *King Kong* — their believability made all the more real by the groundwork done by Knight and his colleagues for the museums.

Every work of art or scientific discovery must have a predecessor, something on which to build a fresh new idea. Charles R. Knight, Willis O'Brien, Gustave Doré, John Martin, and Frank Brangwyn were my heroes, my source of inspiration. Undoubtedly they will continue to inspire kindred souls throughout eternity.

RAY HARRYHAUSEN

My history is very similar to Ray Harryhausen's. We both saw the Willis O'Brien film *The Lost World* in 1925, and we both fell in love with his Knight-inspired dinosaurs. And then when *King Kong* came along in 1933, that was even better, because Kong was fantastic, and the dinosaurs were incredible.

Dinosaurs infested my dreams. We're enchanted with time — when we think of these beasts, these monsters, that lived in the world for so many hundreds of thousands of years, and then vanished, and we think we're going to be here for a long time... Well, if the dinosaurs could vanish from the world, we have to be careful with ourselves.

But when you do excellent things, you live forever. So the work that Charles R. Knight did — it's there forever, and it's going to stay forever.

RAY BRADBURY

Charles Robert Knight was born in Brooklyn, New York on October 21, 1874 to an English father and a mother from Maine. His passion for drawing animals began at age five, when he would copy animals from steel engraving book illustrations. At age six, Knight was struck in his right eye by a stone that left him with permanent corneal damage. Combined with inherited astigmatism, Knight became legally blind and for most of his life he was forced to paint with his good left eye just inches from the canvas.

Despite this handicap, Knight began his formal art training at the Froebel Academy, then continued on at Brooklyn Collegiate and Polytechnic Institute. At twelve the budding young artist attended classes at the Art School of the Metropolitan Museum of Art. Offered work creating designs for a stained glass factory, Knight left home at age sixteen. Knight attended drawing classes at the Art Students League (studying under, among others, George de Forest Brush) and he began to indulge his passion for depicting animal life with morning sketching trips to the Central Park Zoo.

Charles soon found work in Manhattan as an illustrator of children's books. While doing freelance work for *McClure's* magazine he met Rudyard Kipling and Sir Arthur Conan Doyle. Knight began to haunt the American Museum of Natural History's taxidermy department, where he made meticulous studies of various wild animals and their muscular and skeletal systems.

American Museum scientist Dr. Jacob Wortman observed Knight at work and asked him if he could produce a life restoration of a giant prehistoric pig-like mammal named *Elotherium (Entelodon)*. Knight took on the challenge and the result changed his life forever. Combining scientific observation with powerful artistic vision, Charles R. Knight almost immediately became the world's most dominant portrayer of prehistoric animals.

At the American Museum of Natural History, Charles R. Knight met one of the greatest minds in the history of paleontology: Henry Fairfield Osborn. Osborn had just created the Department of Vertebrate Paleontology at the Museum. His 1896 article "Prehistoric Quadrupeds of the Rockies" was published in *Century Illustrated Monthly Magazine* with illustrations by Knight. In that same year *McClure's* sent Knight off on a tour of the great museums and zoos of Europe. In Paris, Knight fell under the spell of the brilliant animal sculpture by the contemporary French artist Antoine Louis Barye, the pioneering and influential leader of a group of animal sculptors who came to be known as *Les Animaliers*. Knight also met with sculptor Emmanuel Fremiet and the world famous academician painter-sculptor Jean-Léon Gérôme. In France and Spain Knight personally examined the magnificent cave paintings at Font-de-Gaume grotto, Cap Blanc and Altamira.

Upon Knight's return to Manhattan, Osborn and scientist William D. Matthew teamed with Knight to create visually dramatic and scientifically accurate displays, bringing the worlds of the museum's prehistoric creatures to life for the general public.

Osborn introduced Knight to the legendary and pioneering paleontologist Edward Drinker Cope ("the greatest conversationalist that ever graced the service of paleontology," according to Knight). Cope was a giant in his field, having discovered 1,115 prehistoric animal species — more than a third of all the known prehistoric species at that time. Knight spent two intensive weeks with Cope, studying Cope's own pencil sketches, learning Cope's philosophies of form and proportions and listening to Cope's speculations in regards to the lives and daily functions of a variety of prehistoric beasts. Cope never got to see the fruits of his meetings with Knight; three weeks later Cope died.

In 1898 Osborn convinced famous banker and Museum patron J. Pierpont Morgan to finance a score of Knight watercolor and sculptural restorations of prehistoric life. Copies were made available to schools and students; the originals were donated to the Museum. For the twelve years following, Knight produced paintings for the American Museum.

In 1900 Knight met and married Annie Humphrey Hardcastle. In 1901 he was commissioned by the U. S. Treasury Department to draw the bison that appeared on the ten dollar bank notes issued to commemorate the Pan-American Exposition held in Buffalo, New York. That same drawing was later reused in 1922 and 1923 on the thirty cent U. S. Postage stamp.

In 1905 daughter Lucy was born; she would ultimately become her father's business manager.

Knight continued to create art for the *Century Illustrated Monthly Magazine* and commissions for the U. S. Fish Commission and U. S. Bureau of Fisheries. He sculpted life-size heads of two African elephants for the Bronx Zoo (where they are still on display), as well as a full-sized tapir and rhinoceros. His work was privately commissioned and collected by many art patrons prominent in New York society.

In the teen years of the twentieth century Knight began the work that would ultimately bring him world fame: his great murals of prehistoric life. The American Museum's Hall of Man murals were completed in 1923; the Natural History Museum of Los Angeles County's Rancho La Brea "Tar Pits" mural was painted in 1925. Knight's largest commission, the twenty eight panels (depicting the pageantry of life on earth from its earliest beginnings, through the Age of Reptiles and on up to the Dawn of Man) for Chicago's Field Museum of Natural History, began in 1926 and was completed in 1930.

Back at the American Museum, Knight painted six more murals. In 1935 he wrote and published *Before The Dawn of History*, illustrated primarily by his Field Museum murals. Knight publicly lectured about prehistoric life and in 1942 published an illustrated article in *National Geographic* magazine. His final series of pictures were twenty-four oil paintings (depicting the succession of early life) painted from 1944 to 1946 (currently in the Natural History Museum of Los Angeles County collection). In 1946 his book *Life Through the Ages* first saw print and in the following year his instructional book *Animal Drawing: Anatomy and Action for Artists* was published. Knight's final book, *Prehistoric Man: The Great Adventure*, was published in 1949.

Dr. George Kunz, an international authority on gems who was instrumental in Knight's Field Museum commission, began planning a Pennsylvania museum completely devoted to Knight: the Kunz Museum of Charles R. Knight's Work. The museum idea fell apart when Kunz died before the ambitious project could be completed. Knight subsequently spent more time with his family, especially with his granddaughter Rhoda. In 1951 Knight painted his final mural for the Everhart Museum in Scranton, Pennsylvania.

If having a lasting influence on other artists is a key criterion for determining the greatness of an artist, then Charles Robert Knight is one of the most important artists of the twentieth century. The profound Knight depictions of prehistoric life that grace the major natural history museums of America visually defined dinosaurs for the rest of the world. The animals he chose to represent were the creatures that became household names to every eight year old across the planet. There was scarcely a dinosaur book published during the first sixty years of the

20th century that did not include examples of Knight's work.

Knight's reconstructions became the basis for how dinosaurs were portrayed in the popular media; from *King Kong, Fantasia* and the animated films of Ray Harryhausen to the Disney theme parks. Knight's work has appeared as toys and on stamps and in comic books. His paintings fired the ambitions of a legion of young people to choose paleontology as their future profession.

Charles R. Knight's magnificent blend of powerful art and good science continues to inspire art, science and imaginations around the world.

WILLIAM STOUT

WILLIAM STOUT *is one of today's premier dinosaur artists. He has done extensive work for film, galleries, museums and comics. He is also one of the very few artists to have traveled to Antarctica under the auspices of the National Science Foundation, and is currently completing the first comprehensive series of paintings illustrating both the past and present life of that continent.*

An Editorial Note

Knight apparently wrote much of this ca. 1940-1945, based on oblique references in the original manuscript to the occupation of France and to a still living Franklin D. Roosevelt. The original manuscript runs a little over sixty thousand words and it contains many redundant passages and digressions that, while occasionally colorful, add little to his narrative. It was a first draft, in other words, and one Knight never returned to. Apparently he lost interest in his story at about the point where it came time to recount his career as the world's premier artist of prehistory and only picked it up again to describe a particularly significant trip later in his life.

What follows is roughly a third of the manuscript's original length, and focuses on Knight's formative years and the events and personalities that shaped them. I have tried to apply as light a touch as possible to his original text, limiting the edits to spelling, punctuation, and factual corrections and occasionally revising and rearranging passages to improve flow. (The latter occurring most often in the sections about his work at Lamb's and his travels abroad.) You'll also find footnotes which will, I hope, add to your appreciation and understanding of Knight's colleagues, life, and times.

JIM OTTAVIANI

Charles R. Knight

AUTOBIOGRAPHY OF AN ARTIST

Childhood

"See the black chicken!"

This remark, according to my father, was the first sentence I ever uttered and would seem in my case to have been prophetic. For even at the early age of two, it shows my interest in living things. The place was a small hotel known as Stockbridge's, on Summit Lake near Central Valley, N. Y. I'd been taken there by my father and mother so that Dad might indulge in his favorite sport of angling for small mouthed black bass.

Sunday was of course Father's free day, so the rest of the week I had to content myself as I might. Occasionally we even went to the Zoo in Central Park where the animals still occupy the same general area in which I first saw them, but then they were housed in a series of rather decrepit buildings which nevertheless persisted until a few years ago. Then our energetic Park Commissioners demolished the ancient structures and built a whole new spick and span Zoo, which in spite of its improved appearance is no better fitted as a home for wild animals. The Museum of Natural History too (at that time only a single red brick building which rose from a pile of broken rocks in the center of Manhattan Square) was naturally a Mecca for a youngster of my peculiar leanings. The long tiled Halls filled to overflowing with glassy-eyed birds and animals, each on its own mahogany base, fascinated me and we had them all to ourselves, as the Museum was not then open to the public on Sundays. Father was J. P. Morgan's[1] private secretary, and the great banker was treasurer of

[1] John Pierpont (J. P.) Morgan (1837–1913), thanks to a head start from his father J. S. Morgan, founded J. P. Morgan & Company. It became one of the most powerful banking

the Museum, so we had weekend access while the public could go only on weekdays. I presume the taxidermy was pretty bad, and many of the specimens were old, cracked and faded, but to me they were a wonderful show, and I vastly enjoyed looking at them. I particularly remember one striking group (our only example) of an Arab camel rider being attacked by a lion. Perhaps other men my age will recall this dramatic piece which for some reason I never clearly understood was in later years given to the Carnegie Museum in Pittsburgh. I always regretted its going as it certainly was a thrilling bit of taxidermy, and only an artist could have done it. The man of course was wax, but his expression as he sat astride the camel's neck to escape the claws of the big cat was well worth seeing. A dead lioness with a little red paint for blood lay at the feet of the camel, and this artificial gore was, I fear, the cause of it being sent away, as it was thought too sensational for a staid institution like our Museum.

❦

At six, my family — father, mother, Silver (our Skye terrier), and Tommy (our big black and white feline), and myself — moved to our new house on Lewis Avenue in Brooklyn Heights, a region at the time very poor in traffic facilities, raw and ugly, but with the advantages of plenty of light and air. Father was great on air. Being stout and as we said then full-blooded, and an Englishman, he felt the heat of this country tremendously and

houses in the world and the world's first billion-dollar corporation. In 1895 it loaned the United States government $62 million in gold to restore the treasury surplus. A book and art collector, Morgan loaned or gave many valuables to the Metropolitan Museum of Art, of which he was president. He was also a benefactor of the American Museum of Natural History and Harvard University.

Most famous for saying "If you have to ask how much it costs, you can't afford it," the more appropriate quote as it relates to Knight's work is "Go as far as you can see; when you get there, you'll be able to see farther."

was never so happy as when he could go swimming in the ocean at Coney Island in the summertime. Our house was a small old brick two story and basement affair with a small frontyard and a big long back yard full of sunlight and ozone — especially in winter when the northwesters simply tore across the back fences and roared so we could hardly sleep at night. Flower beds ran around three sides of our yard and Virginia Creeper covered the high board fences which separated us from our neighbors. It was a grand spot for a small boy and the neighborhood was bright and open with many lots still not built upon, but with houses going up all about us. I rejoiced in my new surroundings, now that I was growing up and could go about more by myself — across the street, around the corner — even to school across lots. It didn't take me long to find congenial companions. My next-door neighbor, Frank North, was a delicate, handsome boy, forever eating dill pickles from a brown paper parcel — sucking the salty juice in a most aggravating fashion, and dropping brine all over the place. This brown paper, a thick but porous product, had a peculiar sweetish taste (I have heard that it contained molasses) and I've certainly seen goats placidly chewing large pieces of it, evidently enjoying its succulent qualities. Frank was great on pickles, but he and I both loved candy too and he could usually wangle two cents from his mother with which we'd rush across the street to the little German grocery and purchase four Everlastings. Two white and two pink, two for him and two for me. Frank was generous, and we'd suck on them for hours. We favored molasses taffy too, and coltsfoot[2] from the drug store. This latter came in long fluted sticks and was soft brown in color and with a peculiar flavor. One never sees it nowadays, but even Father liked the strange exotic taste and used to buy it for me quite often on his way home from the office.

---

[2] Coltsfoot candy was made by boiling fresh leaves of the colt's foot plant and adding sugar to the extract. The roots and leaves of this perennial are also thought to have medicinal value.

When at last I was old enough to go to school, I was sent to a little private neighborhood school on Quincy Street, conducted by the Misses Richardson, two charming and very pretty young ladies who were most kind to me and whom I adored in consequence. I don't remember much about the school, except that one of the children had a sister who was a dancer. I'd never seen a real dancer before and the sight of that graceful little figure clothed in green satin trimmed with white rabbit fur thrilled me through and through. This lovely dark eyed and raven haired little sylph could really dance too; indeed, she was a professional, though naturally that didn't mean anything to me. This realization of beauty was something quite new to me, but I have always felt that the charming active little girl aroused for the first time my love of pretty things.

My eyes, I suppose, had never been of the best, as my father was very near-sighted, and I had inherited his full and astigmatic eyes. But at the age of six I was to suffer a most distressing accident, and one which was to prove a decided handicap to me through life. One day when I was playing with a boy about my own age he carelessly tossed a small pebble which struck me directly in my right eye. The blow threw me to the ground, blood burst from my eye socket, and I was carried home in a dazed condition. The doctor came at once, held up fingers which I counted to see if I still had vision and I was promptly put to bed in a darkened room. Here for six weeks I lay in a sort of misery, very little pain, but most uncomfortable, while dressings of acetate (sugar) of lead[3] were kept continually over my injured optic. I can still smell the disagreeable bitter earthy odor of the acetate as it assailed my nostrils night and day until the inflammation was somewhat reduced and I was at last allowed to come out once more into the light of day — but with a dark patch still over the hurt eye. This was finally removed, and I could see again, apparently almost as well as

---

[3] Lead acetate was used as an astringent to cause shrinkage of mucous membranes or exposed and damaged tissues. Current practice is to avoid contact with the eye altogether.

ever. Real damage however had been done, and the excessive inflammation set up by the blow was later to very seriously affect the vision in my right eye, thus throwing a great amount of extra work upon my left eye, which was already both near-sighted and astigmatic to a marked degree. My sight was, after all, fair, even with these handicaps, and it was not until several years later that I began to realize my inability to distinguish objects clearly at a distance. For me of course it was a catastrophe for in my chosen line as an artist I naturally needed two good eyes and here I was attempting to do difficult and intricate work with only one poor organ at the best. Also I have no doubt that the accident contributed a great deal to my later nervous condition as my vision was always under a strain which reacted upon my entire nervous system. Misfortune, however, of a much more serious kind was soon to overtake our family, for we had lived in the new house only a year or two when at Christmas time my mother suddenly became ill and died in a week from pneumonia. On that last night, as I left her bedside something must have warned her — some inkling that she would never see me again prompted her to call after me

— Good night, Charlie.

— Good night Mommy, I answered.

Fainter and fainter the voice:

— Good night Charlie.

— Good night.

— Good night.

These were her last words to her little boy for in a few hours she was past speaking.

I had made my first trip to England when Mother was living, but under the new conditions Father decided to go again and see his family in Oxford. He had come to this country from the London banking house of J. S. Morgan[4] and Company, and every two or three years J. P. Morgan would give him a three month vacation to see his folks back home. So it was that we found ourselves once more upon the broad Atlantic on the good White Star ship "Germanic," then the crack boat of the line. She was a very long and narrow vessel, a terrific roller in a heavy sea, but fast and up-to-date for her time, reaching Liverpool in ten days out of New York if all went well. I enjoyed the trip with the exception of the excitement caused by a loose front tooth which hanging by a chord of skin I refused to have removed. Howling like a little idiot I danced about our narrow stateroom until the ship's doctor, wise in the ways of children, succeeded in fastening a string around the tooth and the other end to the door knob. Then with a quick jerk out of my mouth popped the little incisor, and it was all over but the congratulations. There were plenty of things on the ship to amuse a small boy, many other children and games galore. Also, one of the sailors decided to raffle off an old straw stuffed iguana (the big South American lizard) and I of course was crazy to take chances upon it. I wasn't lucky and was bitterly disappointed in consequence, but as a matter of fact I was the only person on the boat who really wanted the ugly thing and I would have treasured it as an addition to my Natural History Collection.

Life after we returned home was the usual quiet affair and exceedingly lonesome for me. But one Sunday when we went to church, Father was interested to see a strange lady in our pew. It was a fateful occurrence for all of us because the chance acquaintance so casually begun soon ripened into a more intimate one, and it was not long before Dad and his

---

[4] Junius Spencer (J. S.) Morgan (1813–1890) founded the house of J. S. Morgan & Co. in London, fathered J. P. Morgan, and was a partner of George Peabody, who we'll meet later as the uncle of the renowned paleontologist Othniel Charles Marsh.

. . . I of course was crazy to take chances upon it.

new found friend became engaged. Miss Sarah Davis, about 30 years old at the time, was a very clever young lady and lived with her father and mother on Lafayette Avenue, within a block or two of our house. Father was 42 at the time, and in May, 1882, they were quietly married at the home of her parents.

China painting, then all the rage, she did remarkably well, producing many lovely things in the way of decorated dinner and tea sets. This is a difficult medium, requiring much technical as well as artistic experience, but my stepmother made light of these very obvious difficulties, and went right ahead with her work in a triumphant sort of way. For me, it was a revelation to see her paint, as for the first time in my life I could really look upon an artist at work, and it naturally clarified my own leanings in that direction. From her also I for the first time heard the word "Art" at least so that it carried any real meaning, and she subscribed to the *Art Journal*, a well illustrated art periodical of the day. I read it, and as I read I dreamed, becoming slowly more conversant with the line of endeavor that I was eventually to follow. My stepmother had ideas for me as well, and she encouraged me to draw and paint on all occasions. While under her guidance I actually produced a set of little butter plates decorated with flowers and insects for my Father's birthday. Her studio also had a little what-not in one corner, whereon reposed various curios brought from one of her Cuban trips. Shells, bits of coral, starfishes, and other strange and novel things, upon all of which my youthful eyes feasted with avidity. Indeed in those first few years we got along famously together, but gradually a rift began to widen between us, a rift which grew ever wider as time went on. I am convinced that just plain jealousy played a large part in her dislike of me, though I could not very well help being my father's only child. The very thought seemed to irritate her, particularly as she was childless herself, and overweeningly ambitious and aggressive in the bargain. She was terribly spoiled too, both by her parents and by my father, who was the type that preferred peace always at any price. This weakness she well knew and would always gain her point by making more or less of a scene at the psychological moment. Unfortunately for me I happened to be in her way so that as the years went by we became less and less friendly. If I have seemed to blame my stepmother unduly, one must not infer for a moment that the fault was all hers, because I was undoubtedly very difficult, and like many sensitive only children showed my irritation by being sulky and generally devilish. We just didn't hit it off together and finally kept out of each other's way as much as possible.

So summers of course were difficult, and there really wasn't very much to do around home in the long vacation time, but Father had a friend named Reginald Hazell, who had a place where he and Mother often went in the summer because the bass fishing was excellent. The Hazell place was a real farm several miles from Central Valley and farther east towards West Point. To reach the estate we took the old Erie train to Central Valley where Mr. Hazell's double horse team would meet us, and then followed a long hard drive up and over Bull Hill, a big rise of ground between the station and the farm. Mr. H. was an Englishman born on the West Indian Island of St. Lucia, and his wife was a charming and beautiful lady of Portuguese extraction, Miss Sarah Corvalho. They were a singularly devoted couple, childless, but very hospitable and charming hosts. I suppose I had been to their country place when I was still very young but now at nine years of age I was able to take things in very easily and to much better understand my surroundings.

Of course, it is a very abstruse subject, but as I think back upon the instruction I received in my artistic career, I can recall no single instance when a teacher thought it worthwhile to clarify the necessary steps in the making of a painting. I did, however, [at the Hazell's, and later the Peck's farm in Newtown] receive a great stimulus to the social side of my character, because of my close contact over many years with so many different personalities. This training for an only child was invaluable because it came at a character-forming period of my life. The art of making myself useful and agreeable was rather new to me, but in such a large company of boys and girls it became an absolute necessity as willy-nilly I found myself greatly improved in this most far reaching part of one's development. Fortunately many of my friends at the farm were past masters at this sort of thing, young as they were, and from them I learned a certain expansiveness of manner which I had hitherto lacked in my dealings with others. Also, this led to a decided lessening of my bad habit of introspection, so easily formed by an only child. Indeed, there was no time for such vague and dangerous feelings, all my days being filled from morning until night with such decidedly concrete matters which were really of some importance in the general scheme, and these contributed to a sense of well being quite new in my experience.

Student

The Froebel Academy

In spite of our differences, my stepmother did recognize the very important fact that my only talent was a certain flair for and intense interest in drawing, and she took pains to encourage my efforts in that direction. She also sent me to a charming school newly founded in our neighborhood. This school, known as the Froebel Academy[5], was one of the very first of its kind in America, and boasted a corps of excellent teachers — young ladies of education and refinement thoroughly schooled in the methods of the Great German educator, Froebel. So to the Academy I went forthwith, there to spend several delightful and I believe fruitful years surrounded by congenial and jolly companions, boys and girls of my own age and younger. Miss Mary Laing, our principal, was a woman of superlative accomplishments, kindly, firm, forceful, and highly stimulating to my youthful and impressionable sensibilities. She seemed to grasp at once all my peculiarities, as indeed she did for all the other scholars, and we felt on our part a distinct responsibility to uphold the high standards which she so cleverly set for us. I was a bit old for the younger grades, so I was placed in the higher classes where we didn't actually do the kindergarten routine. Nevertheless there were plenty of

[5] Friedrich Wilhelm August Froebel (1872–1952) invented the kindergarten system. His theories cited self-activity, spiritual and physical training, and pleasant surroundings as all being important aspects in the development of a child. Initially a student of architecture, he designed a set of building blocks that Frank Lloyd Wright used from an early age through the rest of his life.

interesting things for us to do: drawing, clay modeling, map making, sand modeling, history, singing, playing games, all combined with the more prosaic studies of the three R's but without too much stress being laid upon the latter. Indeed, so tactfully was the work diversified that it always seemed like fun to us. Froebel of course was a pioneer in this sort of teaching and believed in much visual instruction and working with the hands, all commonplace today but then quite new and revolutionary as far as America was concerned.

Brooklyn Collegiate and Polytechnic

My Froebel Academy years passed, much to my regret, and I was sent to the Brooklyn Collegiate and Polytechnic Institute. It was a very long distance from our home, several miles, and while I used to ride there in the morning on the old Gates Avenue horse cars, my stepmother decided that I must walk home to get exercise. I got it all right, but I hated taking so much time away from my playmates in our own neighborhood, because at 12 or 14 a boy is just beginning to have real fun out of doors, and there were many boys and girls to make things lively for me. The homework too, of which there always seemed to be an endless amount involving mathematics, hung over me like a pall, especially higher arithmetic, algebra and finally geometry. Algebra was just a blank to me and I never really understood (and don't now, for that matter) just what was the sense in hunting up the letter X so assiduously, and the problems about the hands of the clock and the fellows who left home at the same time and couldn't seem to keep together because one had longer legs...

Geography I liked, and history and grammar, and drawing of course. This latter was a shining light in my education and my teacher, Professor [Constantin] Hertzberg, was very good to me and made my hour every day with him a very pleasant one. He knew little about drawing himself, but allowed me to draw at least from the real thing: heads, animals, and ornaments from plaster casts. Even though this branch of art was Greek to him, and he had us draw with a stump and crayon, a desperately bad medium for a beginner, he was the first to support my interests, and set me on my path of becoming a real artist.

I got along fairly well (except in mathematics, where I was a complete failure) but I stuck it out and plodded along as best I could. One great day occurred, however, during my time at Poly, and that was the big blizzard of '88. It pretty nearly finished me, young and strong as I was, and I shall never forget it. As I recall the date, it was the 12th of March, very late for such a storm, and it had snowed all Sunday night so that by Monday morning when I set off for school the snow was fairly deep and it was blowing a gale and very cold. I walked my usual distance to my friend Rob Sweezey's house, and from there we took the horse car to the school. Neither of us thought anything unusual was going on, and we were surprised and delighted when classes were let out about 11 o'clock and we were told to go home. The storm was really bad by this time and the weary horses had an awful time dragging the heavy street car along the snow-covered tracks. Indeed, when they were within two or three blocks of Rob's (he lived close to the cars) they gave it up, completely abandoning the now snowed in conveyance, and we walked to his house. I still had not felt the real force of the wind, but when I started for my own house, I had to go along Greene Ave. where there were very few houses, and the snow was by this time swirling and blowing so violently into my face that I could hardly breathe. Then for the first time I really became alarmed, and struggled into the house of a friend, Chas. Debevoise (since the great World War he has been General Debevoise) where I secured a knitted cap, which I pulled right down over my nose and eyes. I could see quite clearly through the woolen meshes, and it kept the powdery flakes from my nostrils. In this way I managed to reach

One great day occurred, however, during my time at Poly . . .

home, pretty tired but far from exhausted. Worse and worse grew the great storm, and when Father came home a few hours later, the snow was piled high on our side of the street, and as he waded through the drifts it nearly engulfed him in its feathery whiteness. Finally he got into the house but, although he was a very powerful man, he was so weary that he could not speak for hours. All that night it snowed heavily and when morning came our basement drawing room windows were completely blocked, and an immense drift as high as our front stoop ran right across the street on a gentle slope. We were marooned, for in those days no one had telephones, and not a thing was moving, not even a milk wagon. There was just one vast sea of white in every direction, and we were looking upon the greatest snow in all New York's history[6].

Father couldn't go to business and I couldn't go to school, so we set to work shoveling our way out through the huge drift that blocked our basement entrance. We made very little impression, however, upon that huge mass of icy snow and gave it up as a bad job, using our upper front stoop door and walking right across the street on the top of the drift. Nothing moved in the city for several days, no horsecars, no wagons, and very few pedestrians, as walking was practically impossible. On the second day I do recall our milkman arriving, driving a boat of all things. Where he got it I can't imagine, but it was better than any sleigh, sliding across the top of the big drift with very little trouble.

Gradually the city began to shovel itself out, and we heard that many people in Brooklyn had lost their lives, dying from exhaustion and cold. The snow was ten or twelve feet deep in the big drifts and our street-cleaners simply tunneled under them to make a passageway on the side-

[6] The storm began on Sunday, March 11, and by its end New York City had received 21 inches of snow. Blown about by 70 miles per hour gusts of wind, drifts upwards of 10 ft. paralyzed the city. (New England was even harder hit, with Massachusetts and Connecticut getting more than 50 inches of snow.) The transportation crisis that resulted led to the creation of the New York subway system.

walks. It was a perilous time for many people, but we boys had a wonderful time having snow fights, sledding, and making caves in the huge mounts of slushy snow which now began to melt in earnest. As the thaw actually set in the streets were turned to rivers, and it was weeks before the last evidences of the tremendous snowfall had completely disappeared. I suffer today from the shock of near death that I experienced in the big blizzard, as a deep snow with a high wind subconsciously recalls that fateful time.

The Metropolitan Art School and The Art Students League

So for four years I plodded my weary way back and forth from the Polytechnic. Upon graduation, I entered the Metropolitan Art School, just started in the basement of the big Museum at 81st and 5th Avenue. At the time, about 1888, the Museum consisted of only two buildings and these stood well back in the Park, not coming out to 5th Ave. as they do today. It wasn't really a good place for such a school, as the light was poor, and many of the rooms, though large, were dark and gloomy. There was plenty of room in the vast recesses of the Museum basement for the Muse of Art to spread her wings, but I fear her broad pinions didn't carry her very far along the hallowed road under those adverse conditions. Everything looked bright to me, however, under the glow of a brand new experience, and I entered on my career there with tremendous zest and enthusiasm. For here I was to really study art, something which had always attracted me, and there were to be no more lessons in geometry and no homework.

I also joined the Art Students League, where I studied cast drawing at night, so my time was now very much taken up — too much so for my own good as it proved later. The Art Students League in those days was situated on 23rd Street over stables near 3rd Avenue. It was dingy and dirty enough in all conscience, and the lights at night were mere flickering little gas jets which gave off a strange yellow glow but didn't do much towards dispelling the surrounding gloom. The scholars, at least in the antique class at night, were mostly women, a good many of them being southerners and glad to escape their home towns for a while and study a bit in New York. They were all older than I, and were a pretty serious but very naive lot, quite different from my Metropolitan acquaintances. I was a raw beginner, having no real knowledge of the principles of light and shade, not what constituted drawing in any way. Charcoal was our accepted medium, and it is a difficult one at first but one soon gets the hang of it and learns to love the beautiful transparent shadows and delicate contours that it makes possible. Casts of heads, hands, full length figures and busts made up our list of models, and they were all difficult and complicated to a degree. Really at first they were far beyond my capabilities, whose study hitherto had been so limited. Many of the heads were from Classic or Renaissance originals, exquisite works of art, pure and majestic in outline and beautifully set off by the shadows they cast. As a matter of fact only an expert who had previously drawn from life could have done these splendid models full justice, but we tackled them with no thought of failure. As in all art classes, there was a vast difference between the best and the worst work. Some of the older men and women did fine things while the rest of us put out some pretty poor stuff. Drawing had always been my forte, so I didn't do so badly considering my lack of experience, but of course my work couldn't compare with the best by a long shot.

Our professor was Willard L. Metcalf[7], a splendid big black haired

[7] The cantankerous Willard L. Metcalf (1858–1925) was one of "The Ten American Painters" (a sort of academy of American Impressionism) that broke away from the Society of Academic American Artists to exhibit on their own.

During the brief time (1890/91–1892) he taught at the Art Students League Metcalf

and black bearded figure of a man with a gruff and (to me) unpleasant manner. He had just returned from Paris and was flushed with success and occasional liquid stimulants, so that he didn't really take much interest in us poor art students, but I presume he needed the money. At the time he was a figure painter, which will be news to many because later he became very celebrated (and justly so) for his beautifully drawn and painted landscapes. He was a most accomplished technician, and I have always envied him his direct and adequate techniques and his splendid sense of composition. Personally, as I say, I didn't take to him, but I did appreciate his excellent if severe, ruthless and sophisticated criticisms, which were something quite new to me. Coming as he did direct from Paris he knew what was what in figure drawing and his line of talk was an eye-opener to me. Such things as values, correct construction, contours, and the way the shadows fall across the surface of the white cast were all new in my experience.

also did illustration jobs. He apparently detested it and invested little of himself in the work, instead adopting A.B. Frost's popular style. His lack of enthusiasm showed. Because of the lack of likeness, authenticity of costume, and absence of dramatic posture, Robert Louis Stevenson said the following about Metcalf's work on his story "The Wreckers": "The series...might have illustrated any story (or nearly any story) ever written." Fortunately for all concerned, his prominence as a landscape painter steadily increased to the point where he no longer had to work for the magazine market. For an overview of his life and work, see Elizabeth De Veer's *Sunlight and Shadow: The Life and Art of Willard L. Metcalf* (NY: Abbeville Press, 1987).

Craftsman

During my second year at the school (when I was sixteen) the church decorating firm of J. and R. Lamb sent a representative to the Museum in search of several young fellows who might be useful in their shops. Fortunately for me I was one of two chosen, my companion being Arthur D. Meeker, a very clever draughtsman who had studied with me in the design class. He was a tall, thin, shy, and very reserved young man, exceedingly neat and accurate in his work, and a find for any concern where precision and beautiful drawing were prime requisites. I still retained my place in the Museum classes and the League, and this combined with working part time at Lamb's engaged me in the dangerous adventure of burning the candle at both ends. My affairs at home were not too prosperous. My stepmother becoming increasingly jealous of me and more and more impossible in every way, and the long pull into the wilds of Brooklyn after my evening at the League in no wise helped my failing strength and spirits. It just couldn't go on, so that one day after an unusually disagreeable fracas at home I announced that I was leaving and going to New York to live with one of my art school friends, Charlie Hubbell and his mother, a widowed lady who seemed glad to have me as a companion to her son.

Joseph and Richard Lamb's establishment at 59 Carmine Street (a continuation of lower Sixth Avenue below 3rd Street) was a most fascinating place for me. As I said, in those days the firm was prominent in the field of church decoration, and there were several different departments which took care of the various types of furnishings used in ecclesiastical work. Chief among them was the stained glass department, but they also had stone, brass, wood and mosaic sections, as well as an embroidery division. In short, everything that was employed by churchmen to make their houses of worship comfortable, artistic and effective. The older members of the firm were Englishmen who had come to this country long before my time and established themselves in what was now a prosperous business. With them in the firm were four younger men, Charles, Fred, and Cesy being Joseph's boys, while young Joe was Richard's son. My particular boss was Fred, a handsome curly-haired and bearded fellow, just come back from Paris where he had studied for several years and who had only lately been placed in charge of designing for the stained glass shop. He and I at once became great friends and my work at Lamb's was always done under the pleasantest of social relations. Charles Rolliston Lamb, Fred's brother, was head of the mosaic shop with a large staff of Italian mosaic and marble workers under him. He was a very dynamic person, rushing about usually with his derby hat on the back of his head, his heavy curly bang very much to the front (literally) and his voice easily heard above the noise of the shop as he told the workmen what was what in mosaic. The two older men attended to all the other departments and looked after the finances as well. These two brothers were both most interesting characters and diametrically unlike in every way, both physically and mentally, yet they always managed to get on well together in spite of occasional differences of opinion.

Our stained glass "studio" existed in name only as the actual place was a mean, dark little shop that had formerly been a Chinese laundry. The real shop, that is where the glass was cut and the windows made, was in another still more gloomy place just across the street. Our studio was a very small affair with one large and one small window, and the light was very poor and fitful. A tiny stove did its best to keep us warm in winter without much success, and I disliked the surroundings intensely. Certainly the modern artisan, working as he does in clean well-lighted and sanitary surroundings, can have but little idea of the depressing conditions under which even high class men worked in those far off days. The neighborhood was filthy, with dirty cobblestoned streets, mostly the poorest type of drinking Irish, and still dingier and dirtier tenement houses. There was a saloon on almost every corner, and to these havens many times a day came low ragged men and women with beer pails which they filled and took home to imbibe the contents at their leisure. Whiskey too was consumed in great quantities, and the sordidness of my surroundings came as rather a shock to my already jaded nerves. Everything and everybody was so down and out, forlorn and miserable looking. Just across the street was an old red brick church building, abandoned by its former congregation and now used as a shelter by the Salvation Army and a place from which they could oversee the people of the neighborhood. Every night hordes of dreary old bums were taken in by these heroic people, fed and given a night's lodging, paying for it by cutting up a few bits of kindling in the morning. How or why young men and women chose to take up this kind of charity for practically no material benefits I never could tell, but even in that tough neighborhood the Salvation lassies would walk right into the saloons alone, distribute their pamphlets, and were never insulted so far as I know. They seemed totally unafraid, buoyed up by their faith, and were our only bright spots in an otherwise dismal environment. Quite often we'd have excitements — a fire perhaps, or some woman shrieking "murder" at the top of her lungs. No one ever paid the least attention to these ear piercing wails and even I became callous at last and let the woman be murdered for all I knew without ever looking up from my work.

I was intensely interested and too busy to give more than a passing thought to these matters, the business being along more intriguing lines than I had imagined in even my most sanguine moments. It was a very prosperous time for stained glass work and orders came thick and fast to the firm. Very little of it ($12 a week, to be exact) flowed in my direction, yet this meager stipend was looked upon with envy by my less fortunate friends, whose salaries were pitifully small compared with what they would be nowadays. Yet it sufficed not only to pay my board and room at Mrs. Hubbell's but also to buy myself occasional clothes and little luxuries. I was now sixteen, not very old and not very strong-nerved, but I enjoyed the work and stuck to it with much enthusiasm. Engrossed in what was to me a pleasant pastime I got on surprisingly well with my boss, Fred Lamb, and we used to have jolly times together, as he recalled his student days in Paris and his work in the various ateliers in the great city on the Seine. At that time I had never seen Paris although my visits to England with Father had prepared me for the long sea voyage. His glowing accounts directed my attention to the pleasures to be met with in *la belle France,* and I mentally vowed to make a trip there some fine day.

My special work at Lamb's was making watercolor sketches for the stained glass windows, and these sketches would afterwards be submitted to individuals or committees who would pay for the finished windows when the work was completed. Many and various were the subjects which I tackled, though as a rule Fred Lamb preferred to do the figure sketches himself. Flowers (passion flowers, lilies, roses) and stained glass trees and flowers of no botanical significance, animals, birds, various and sundry objects, books, keys, etc., all were within my province, and many of the big windows were filled with just abstract ornament which I drew with great facility from my long practice at the Art School. We often had copies of famous paintings to translate into glass and the prime favorite picture among these seemed to be Hofmann's[8] "Christ in the Temple." We all recall the picture I think, the beautiful young Christ standing surrounded by a number of shrewd, worldly old

---

[8] Heinrich Hofmann (1824–1902) was born in Germany and studied in Dusseldorf and at the Antwerp Academy. He settled in Dresden, where he was a professor of art as well as a

Rabbis, who are listening intently to the words of Our Lord, words given a new meaning in the mouth of the Divine stripling and intoned with an inspiration that astounds his heavens. I suppose the picture would today be called old-fashioned, unsophisticated and mushy. Yet it was the most popular of all our religious subjects, and I don't know how many times and in how many different sizes we executed it during my years at Lamb's. On many occasions Fred made original cartoons for wealthy patrons, but the bulk of our figure work lay in the reproduction of many celebrated pictures of religious subjects. Church committees weren't always easy to handle, but as a rule Fred gradually smoothed out all difficulties in a quite masterly manner.

Though it has quite gone out of fashion nowadays, in my time all fine windows were executed in opalescent glass, an American invention which possessed great artistic possibilities in the hands of a master, and the fine windows of that time designed by such men as John La Farge[9], [Frederic] Crowninshield, Louis Tiffany and others will always

painter. Most famous for idealized scenes from the life of Christ, his 1882 painting titled "Christ in the Temple" was Hofmann's most frequently reproduced work.

[9] Not as well known today as his contemporary Louis Tiffany, John La Farge (1835–1910) was not only an innovator in stained glass but also wielded tremendous influence on post-Civil War America's attitudes towards world art and culture. He wrote a number of books, including *An Artist's Letters from Japan* (1897), *Reminiscences of the South Seas* (1911), and *One Hundred Masterpieces of Painting* (1912), and was quite modern in his avoidance of the romantic and dramatic in his landscapes. Though now considered one of the founders of the mural movement in America, he was ahead of his time, and as a result his paintings were almost completely unappreciated while he was alive.

Impatient with the lack of understanding by his critics and the public at large, he turned to other media, especially glass. In 1879 he invented a technique of fusing small bits of it to create opalescent glass, which allowed for the creation of images that previously could only be achieved by hand-painting. He was able to create highlights and shadows via irregularly made glasses and was a master at rendering realistic images via effects within the glass rather than by paint on the glass. He was typically involved in every step of a window's production, from cartoon to watercolor sketch to choosing and sorting the pieces. La Farge and Tiffany were friends, but that friendship ended with their dispute

. . . as a rule Fred gradually smoothed out all difficulties in a quite masterly manner.

be cherished for their beautiful color effects and original conception. This wonderful glass came in large sheets, usually more or less heavily corrugated in cooling, and presented most enchanting and varied color schemes which the skillful designer adapted to his needs in a most ingenious manner. One must realize that stained glass is the only artistic medium which employs the light of the sun to give the colors their full value and it consequently has a brilliance attainable in no other way. Who has not sat enthralled in some quiet cathedral and watched the glorious light filter through the many hued windows set in the somber walls of dark gray stone? To be sure, the old glass of Europe was of a different kind from that which we used, individual pieces being more transparent and simpler in color and their brilliant reds, blues, greens and yellows in juxtaposition and in many small pieces imparted a scintillating and magnificent effect to these old and (now, alas, very rare) examples of the glazier's art. But they, beautiful as they are, cannot compare in variety of color scheme with the better examples of our own opalescent glass, so that while lovely windows are again being done today in the antique style they cannot from the very nature of things be so personal in their treatment. Very little paint was used in our windows, with the exception of the flesh in the figure pieces. The effects were obtained by careful selection of certain pieces of glass whose color agreed with the sketch which was used as a model. In this way extremely brilliant and glowing tones were possible, exquisite skies, clouds and foliage all transmitting the unsullied light of the sun in a most charming manner.

I still maintain that this technique and the glass that made it possible gave to your true artist an infinite scope in his treatment of a subject. For example John La Farge, a master of color, gloried in deep rich tones

over the rights to use opalescent glass in windows. For more about this often overlooked master, see *John La Farge: Essays*, by Henry Adams, et al. (NY: Abbeville Press, 1987).

of blue-green and purple, while Crowninshield[10] did wonderful things in red and yellow and gold. Louis Tiffany[11], always a seeker after original effects, set up some of the loveliest conceptions ever done in glass and there were many other artists of note who devoted their skill and time to this delightful line of artistic expression.

᙭

To the layman the making of a stained glass window is a rather mysterious performance, and few realize the vast amount of time, labor and skill that enters into the production of such a difficult piece of work. Naturally I am referring now to figure windows or windows with complicated ornaments or foliage in their composition. First of all comes our sketch, done either in oil or watercolor and embodying in a rather feeble way the designer's conception of the finished effect of the glass.

[10] Frederic Crowninshield (1845–1918), was the grandson of Benjamin Williams, a U.S. Senator and Secretary of the Navy under Presidents Madison and Monroe. Crowninshield graduated from Harvard and followed his university education by studying water color and oils in England, France, and Italy. His first work exhibited in public was an allegorical portrait group sent to the Paris Salon of 1878. In later years he devoted his attention to landscapes, mural painting and stained glass.

[11] Before their falling-out, La Farge and Louis Comfort Tiffany (1848–1933) financed the experimental production of opalescent window glass at Louis Heiht's glass house in Brooklyn, leading to opalescent glass with multiple colors mixed in the same sheet, confetti glass, streamer, ridged, and drapery glass, and a number of other exotic variations. *Behind the Scenes of Tiffany Glassmaking: The Nash Notebooks*, by Leslie Hayden Nash (NY: St. Martin's Press/Christie's Fine Arts Auctioneers, 2001) offers an excellent look at the day-to-day work of Tiffany's shop.

Tiffany began his career as a painter in the 1860s, and like so many other artists mentioned here, from La Farge to Gérôme to Knight himself, he traveled extensively, always studying the play of light on natural subjects. This travel also introduced Tiffany to medieval and Roman glass, and his reputation was made via stained glass windows commissioned from him by Mark Twain, Cornelius Vanderbilt, and the White House.

The design is often a matter of long discussion between the artist and some person or committee who have been delegated to see that the work is carried out satisfactorily. It may be original or copied, as I have said, from some well known painting. To make the sketches I employed a curious technique by means of which we hoped to indicate an effect of stained glass with its flickering lights and shades of color, as well as a suggestion of lead lines between the various pieces. After the sketch had been submitted and approved my next task was to make the full sized drawing, no matter how large or how small that might be, and in this drawing all the lead lines were very carefully indicated. In our technique these lead lines and the more or less artistic manner in which they were placed were a very important part of my work because they were the outlines of the form and served to make the silhouettes of the whole design. Awkward lead lines made for poor drawing, while beautifully directed ones accentuated the shapes we wished to show. So it was that I devoted all the skill I had to the making of these full sized cartoons, because they were the patterns from which the glass was to be cut.

When finished I turned the drawing over to the glass cutter who promptly made a tracing of it showing each line in its exact place. Then began the real work of the cutter, who, by the way, was usually a Scotchman or an Englishman. The final effect of the finished window depended on his skill in choosing the proper colors and his ability to cut the delicate and complicated shapes in the best way. For this skilled labor many of the men even in my day received 5, 6, even 8 dollars a day, good wages for the time. But for that they were expected to do excellent work, one cutter methodically selecting, cutting and replacing each cut out shape of glass upon the paper design until the whole is completed and the window, as far as the glass is concerned, lies flat before him on the table. (Had there been figures in the design, the flesh of all these, hands, feet, and faces, would have had to be painted in china colors, and fired several times, before the pieces were inserted into the finished design.) Now comes the leading, done by another man but also requiring technical skill. This T-shaped lead, when properly cut and fastened along the edges of every piece of glass, binds the whole design together and gives it the peculiar character which so distinguishes it. As a last touch to make the window complete a cement paste is smeared over the outer surface of the window and rubbed into the tiny cracks between the lead and the glass by the pressure of a stiff scrubbing brush. This waterproofed the entire window and the job was complete.

Illustrator

Upon his father's death from a stroke, Knight became so depressed that he had to leave work at Lamb's: "It was strange, but I had lost all my former interest in everything. I suffered no pain, but a deadly staleness, as I described it, held me fast in its clutches."

He eventually recovered, thanks in part to another stay at a farm in upstate New York, and returned to the city...

...but at that time no one had anything to do and they were not taking on any men during the depression that was sweeping the country. It was a hopeless outlook, though I was in no real jeopardy, having my few thousand dollars inheritance which I could use in an emergency, and my expenses very few. Yet I felt that at my age I could ill afford to sit down and spend my tiny patrimony doing nothing. Suddenly it occurred to me, why not try to get some illustrations to do? Animals preferably, as I had studied them so long and arduously. It was a happy thought and I acted upon it at once, starting out the next day on a new line of endeavor. The publishing houses — *Harper's, McClure's,* the American Book Company, and many others — were receptive but noncommittal. Yet they were not actually discouraging in their remarks. So I persevered, going back again and again to see editors, sub-editors and just office boys.

Finally, and on a lucky day for me, I went to the American Book Company a second time and there met an assistant editor, Mr. Laurie Smith. This handsome young man, dark, with deep black eyes and curling hair, received me most graciously, listened to what I had to say, and then promptly offered me several small illustrations to do for children's readers. I was delighted. Here at last was an opening, and I tried to take advantage of it. He offered me $25 apiece for the pictures, which was very good pay, as they each took me less than a week to do. I trod on air all the way to Harlem, told my good Mrs. Hubbell and my other friends and acquaintances all about it, and we had a jolly time over my good luck.

It was wonderful, and my stock rose tremendously in the estimation of my friends. So began a long series of drawings for Mr. Smith, and never have I met a man who was more easily pleased and who was anxious to pay me all I asked and more. This sort of work gave me a tremendous mental stimulus, as it was just what I had always wanted to do without knowing just how to get at it. Perforce I had been obliged to go into animal drawing, my own particular forte, giving up for good salaried positions of any kind and embarking on what was really to be my life career. Fate must have willed this singular change in my affairs — fate and nervous prostration combined, as it was the latter that had really caused me to stop my drawing at Lamb's and begin again in an entirely different field.

I was now an illustrator, going about from place to place in search of extra orders. I had not long to wait, as I soon met S. S. McClure, whose splendid magazine was just starting. He introduced me to August Jacenes, his editor, and from him I quickly received an order to do an article on poisonous snakes written by the French savant, Prof. Calmette[12]. Other articles came along later, including an assignment to do a series of drawings showing life behind the scenes at the circus. I met several

---

[12] *McClure's* doesn't list its editors so I've not been able to verify Knight's memory here, though it is accurate when it comes to recalling that the magazine published stories by Sir Arthur Conan Doyle, Rudyard Kipling, and other notables. The article about Calmette's work features beautiful and dramatic illustrations on each page, giving ample evidence that Knight had already developed the skills that would make him famous.

noted men at *McClure's* in the course of a few years, including Sir Arthur Conan Doyle, [Rudyard] Kipling and others, none so celebrated then as they later became, but S. S. McClure had a very discerning eye for new and promising writers and many of his early finds proved themselves men of parts in the literary field. McClure himself was a live wire, a man of tremendous energy, and the place had the air of a newspaper office. Everything was marked "Rush" with a thick blue pencil and in a short time the magazine had a big circulation and was a great success, though in the years to come it was to go steadily downward until it ceased being published altogether.

McClure's was not my only illustration mainstay among the magazine publishers, as I still did much work for the American Book Co. and now I was to meet the editors at the Century Co. in Union Square. In distinct contrast to the bustle and furor at *McClure's*, at the Century Co. an air of serene literary calm pervaded their beautiful quiet rooms. Tastefully furnished with pictures and objects of art, as one strolled into their sacred precincts they gave one a sense of relief from ordinary cares and worries. Charming and very highly educated young ladies met one at the entrance doors and your name was carried politely to the Art Editor.

Alexander Drake had charge of that department when I knew them, and he was the most affable, able and kindly individual I ever worked for in the business. He was tall, somewhat stooped, with full, nearsighted eyes behind glasses, short sideburns, and a smooth, soft ingratiating manner which gave one a sense of ease and security in his presence. It was a pleasure to work for him because he made you feel that the Century was delighted to have work by such a clever fellow as yourself, and the price, well, that could be very easily arranged to suit, he was certain. Never have I enjoyed working for anyone as I did for this scholarly and distinguished man. If I wished to go to Bermuda I could make several pictures for them which paid my way and something over, and my pictures were returned to me to dispose of in any way I saw fit. It was an ideal arrangement for a fellow of my temperament and a visit to Mr. Drake's office was a treat. He was a collector of many things — old hat boxes, bottles and brasses being among his little fads, and to this pleasant pastime he devoted the discerning quality of a most discriminating taste. His brasses in particular were well known to all collectors, and he had a superb and valuable assortment of lovely curios and instructive objects all in that gleaming metal, and all carefully polished and cared for. Ship models were also acquired by him, and he had a most beautiful one in his office. He loved stories and could listen to and tell them by the hour. Indeed, I often wondered how he ever accomplished any work, but Alexander Drake knew his business in a way few men have ever known it, and his way of doing things was always his own. For me, who loved the things he loved, my trips to the Century were milestones in my illustration career.

Animal drawing had now become a kind of specialty with me, and I had quite a reputation in that line, young as I was. But domestic animals were not, strange to say, always easy to find as models. In my work for the American Book Co. I had many times to go out of the city to get what I wanted in this line. Colts and calves and lambs, bulls and bears were not to be found walking the streets of N.Y. except possibly the latter animals and they were confined to the Wall Street area and had only two legs. The Zoo in Central Park was then the only place I could go to draw wild animals, and the houses were old and very inconvenient places in which to work, as space was so limited in front of the cages. Nevertheless it was my one chance at living models, and I took advantage of it. Lions and tigers were always my favorites, and at different times we had some fine specimens of the big cats. I learned to be careful when I was working as the claws of a tiger can do terrific damage unless one is very watchful, and blood poisoning is apt to result from even a small scratch.

I learned to be careful when I was working . . .

Most horned animals are dangerous, as they can strike with great force, and a blow from the antlers of a big stag is a serious matter.

I never petted the animals nor fooled with them in any way, and to this I attribute my freedom from accidents during my long years of studies in various zoological gardens. I recall a very dramatic case incident which occurred in this same zoo and which involved the keeper who had charge of Chiko and Johanna, two big chimpanzees belonging to Barnum's circus. These two great apes inhabited a big, roomy cage in the basement of the old Arsenal Building during the winter, and a special man was delegated to look after them. He slept in the same apartment with this dour and savage pair and at night was quite alone in the lower part of the building. One fateful evening he was about to retire, and, having taken off his heavy shoes, walked over to the apes' cage to have a last look at his charges. Somehow he drew too close to the cage, and Chiko suddenly grasped him by the throat and drew him up against the bars. Feebly resisting he threw out his hands to push himself away only to have the big monkey seize one hand in his powerful paw. In desperation the poor fellow pressed his stockinged foot against the bars and Johanna, who had now joined her mate, instantly pinioned his foot in the same way. It was a terrible predicament, held as in a vise by the ruthless creatures and slowly being choked. To make matters worse they proceeded to bite off pieces of his fingers and toes, spitting them out as one does orange pips. Finally, with true simian indifference, and when the tortured victim was almost unconscious, they suddenly dropped him in a fainting condition to the floor where he lay for some time unable to move. At length, summoning all his strength, he called for help and was rescued in the nick of time. I saw him weeks afterward when he hobbled into the taxidermist shop in the Museum, his hands and feet still swathed in bandages, and if ever I saw a human being look as though he had been through Hell, he was that man.

Artist

From the foregoing incident one may judge that I had good reason to be careful and keep a weather eye open for just such contingencies. I thoroughly enjoyed my task, however, as it kept me in the open air much of the time, and I was a free lance into the bargain. I redoubled my studies of all sorts and kinds of animals, went a great deal to the American Museum of Natural History and became acquainted with my future *confreres* in the various departments. It seems strange as I look back upon my life how a set of circumstances, none of my own making, had gradually forced me into doing animals professionally, when I had really only intended to draw them as an amateur. Slowly but surely I was drifting into my future career as an animal painter, and I was exceedingly fortunate in my friendships with different men at the Museum; men who were willing to help a serious worker like myself, because they were themselves hard and constant toilers, delving profoundly into the secrets of animal anatomy, proportion and psychology. Everything seemed to come my way in those days, or at least a fair amount of work and a moderate income. As in my younger days when Father had taken me to the Museum, I again haunted the halls of that great institution, gleaning what I could from the treasures they contained. To be sure, taxidermy as an art was still in its infancy, but favorable signs of great improvement were just beginning to make themselves evident. A great group of American bison was just being set up at the Museum, mounted under the direction of Jenness Richardson, a clever, delicate man who passed away with consumption shortly after I knew him. He had as his chief assistant a young fellow named John Rowley, a far cleverer man than himself, and this energetic individual at once assumed the carrying on of the work and made a name for himself in the years to come. John was a strange type, small, exceedingly thin, with a long very slim neck, surmounted by a great dome shaped head, and funny little pinched features. A pair of brilliant gray eyes counteracted the effect of his physical appearance, and within that large round skull originated some very clever and practical schemes in the art of taxidermy[13].

In 1893, almost anyone stuffed animals; that is, they literally inserted into the prepared skin all the excelsior[14] possible to build up the form, then sewed up the seams in the legs and belly. Large, staring glass eyes were set in place, the hair given a good brushing, and behold — a pretty poor imitation of a living creature. One can imagine how dreadful was this finished product in light of today's superior knowledge, but few people knew anything about these things 50 years ago, and cared less. In consequence, much atrocious work was foisted upon an ignorant public by a body of men whose colossal conceit and lack of true insight could produce nothing but the poorest examples of the taxidermist's art. John Rowley devoted all his talents to the improvement of this sad state of affairs, and as he was exceedingly able technically as well as artistically, the results were revelations to many people who for the first time saw before them at least a fair representation of a living creature. I have always considered myself fortunate that I was present when these first promising efforts were just beginning to materialize, because in the years since that time I have seen a whole new science of taxidermy rise to full completion. Curiously enough and quite without premeditation, I was preparing my-

[13] John Rowley (1866–1928) wrote two influential books on the subject: *The Art of Taxidermy* (1898) and *Taxidermy and Museum Exhibition* (1925). The only pictures of him I found showed him in profile, wearing a hat, but even these indicate that Knight was right about him being odd looking.

[14] Excelsior consists of fine, curled wood-shavings, and was used as stuffing or packing material not only for taxidermy but for furniture such as mattresses and sofas.

self for the unique branch of art that I was to follow for many years. I remember well the little dirty taxidermist's shop as it existed in those days at the Museum. It was just a two story wooden lean-to jutting out from the northeast corner of the original Museum building, close to the main entrance on that same corner. We used to wait eagerly for specimens to arrive from the old Central Park Zoo, usually in pretty poor condition — emaciated, crippled, and otherwise not very good subjects for study. Nevertheless, we got busy on them right away. I drew close-ups of noses, eyes, paws, and ears, and the boys made plaster casts before and after skinning. Then we'd study the muscles, and the bony structure, and again I'd draw assiduously from the defunct and sometimes smelly cadavers.

It was a real anatomy course — a dead tiger, a lion, a queerly formed kangaroo or a much disheveled macaw or pelican, they all came one after another, under our careful scrutiny, and we learned a lot about their forms and proportion, all of which helped us in our respective jobs. I very soon found that when I again drew from the living animals, my bone and muscle studies had given me a far deeper insight into their general construction than I had formerly possessed, and that I was better able to interpret the position and flow of the muscles as the animals moved about in their cages. It's a very difficult thing even under the best circumstances to make a good drawing of a living animal, but without this preliminary study it is certainly impossible to produce a satisfactory picture. So I worked at my art, illustrating, drawing from life at the Art School, and making always my paintings and drawings from the real animal whenever possible.

To many of us, very important things in our career occur quite casually and I was no exception. John Rowley and I had become very good friends, so that one day when I entered the shop he said, "There was a man named Dr. Wortman here yesterday, from upstairs in the Fossil Department, and he was looking for someone who might make him a drawing of a pre-historic animal. I said I believed you could do it, so why don't you go up and see him?" Thus, in the most prosaic way imaginable I was introduced to a set of men whose interest and encouragement eventually opened up for me a momentous period in my life's work, and created a whole new field of research and study into which I could delve to my heart's content. Dr. Jacob Wortman[15] was not a very prepossessing individual — beetle browed, with coarse, straight, dark hair and a Vandyke beard, his mien was that of a serious medical man, as indeed he was, having been a physician before becoming interested in Paleontology. He specialized in teeth, and what those teeth could tell in the story of evolution, and was an expert in his line. I was courteously greeted and asked whether I thought I could make a restoration of a fossil animal. My modest reply was that I would try, and what was the beast he had in mind? It proved to be a curious pig-like animal — *Elotherium*, with special and peculiar characters which set it off more or less in a class by itself. I completed the drawing satisfactorily in black and white watercolor, and it still hangs in the Museum by the specimen. The date is 1894. Thus without realizing it I had stumbled on a kind of work which was to occupy much of my time for the next 40 years or more. Dr. Wortman was pleased with my initial attempt, gave me more work to do, and later I met Henry Fairfield Osborn, then a professor at Columbia who was taking over the senior position in the Department of Paleontology[16].

[15] Jacob Wortman (1856–1926) was just as expert as Knight makes him out to be, though a great deal more handsome than he remembers! He did excellent field work over the course of many decades, and eventually became the first Curator of Vertebrate Paleontology at the Carnegie Museum of Natural History.

In 1899 Wortman discovered three specimens of the sauropod *Diplodocus* at the Morrison Formation in Wyoming (now known as Dinosaur National Monument), one of which was designated as the "type specimen" — the example by which all others of that species are evaluated — of *Diplodocus carnegii*.

[16] Henry Fairfield Osborn (1857–1935) was the first curator of the vertebrate paleontology department at the American Museum of Natural History. He was Museum president

My modest reply was that I would try, and what was the beast he had in mind?

Professor O. was a totally different type from Dr. Wortman, and had all the suavity of manner of a cultured and aristocratic gentleman. We got on famously together and I like to think that we were mutually helpful as we talked over various projects for the exhibition of the fossil skeletons, and how we might make models and paintings of them for the edification of the general public. The Museum's collection of fossils at the time, particularly the vertebrates, was rather meager, and there were practically no fully mounted skeletons of the animals we had under discussion. Indeed, few museums in the world at the time could boast of more than a very few fossil creatures actually set up in approximately natural position. For the most part, collections consisted of separated bones, very interesting to specialists but totally lacking in popular appeal. Also, not even an experienced scientist could properly visualize the finished effect of an accurately mounted skeleton. Indeed, the collecting of prehistoric animals in the U. S. was still in a very primitive state, and the wonderful technique which has since been so successfully employed was then unknown in field operations.

Professor Osborn was young, well trained and enthusiastic, and he wished to make a fine showing of things Prehistoric for his newly acquired department. Above all, he was something of a naturalist and an artist at heart, and had a great appreciation of all things living and

Morris K. Jessup's second choice for the job — Othniel Charles Marsh was the first, since Jessup hoped to acquire Marsh's team of collectors and his vast collection as well. Osborn eventually became president of the museum himself, and by hiring the best fossil collectors (Barnum Brown, Roy Chapman Andrews), preparators (Adam Hermann, Charles Christman), cultivating relationships with wealthy patrons (J.P. Morgan), purchasing some of the best collections (Edward Drinker Cope's), and financing some of this out of his own pocket, he made the Museum the best and most exciting place in America to find fossils...above ground.

The American Museum of Natural History's Book of Dinosaurs and Other Ancient Creatures by Joseph Wallace (NY: Simon & Schuster, 1994) provides an enjoyable introduction to Osborn and the institution he brought to international prominence.

beautiful. Also, he saw the necessity for embarking on some plan or method of installation that would interest the intelligent layman in his fast-growing gallery of fossil creatures. We saw eye-to-eye from the first in these matters and realized the possibilities ahead of us and set to work with a will to make our schemes a success. Naturally, under the guidance of such an inspired leader the youthful Department forged quickly ahead, attracting several brilliant young men as assistants in various branches of the science. While the laboratories hummed with the sound of drills, scrapers and mallets wielded by the skillful hands of numerous excellent preparators, specimens of all sorts, shapes and sizes poured in from the field expeditions, several of which were out most of the summer. Big and little bones were unearthed from their long rest beneath the soil of some western state and later assembled and placed on exhibition. It was an inspiring time for all of us — we were young, strong and energetic, filled with enthusiasm and determined to make our halls the finest in the world.

Paris

I was fortunate in my choice of a home in New York because my landlady as I have said was like a second mother to me, and now I learned that she had two nieces in Paris who had lived in Europe for years, knew French well, and how to live cheaply in the big town. What more could one ask? I was working at my drawings, had a tiny income from this work, and best of all, my good friend and chum, Charles Peck (a cousin of Charles Peck in Newtown) was willing and anxious to go with me, and I even convinced Mrs. Hubbell that she should come along too and enjoy the fun. We sailed on an old Dutch boat, stopping at Boulogne, where we disembarked, and immediately found ourselves amid the terrific confusion of a French seaport town. As usual the train people acted as if they had never heard of Paris and that this was the first boat that had ever docked in the port. They apparently hadn't the slightest idea in which train we were to be placed, nor had they any desire to find out. In short, it was just French, right from the first.

The Paris of '96 was a lovely city and the country of *la belle France* enchanted my youthful eyes. I saw then why it was that French landscapes always seemed to have a grayish silvery tone, for truly that was the effect one absorbed when looking at the delicately green trees and the gently rolling country that so intrigued one's artistic imagination. (Later, when I went to England, I was struck by the contrast in the color of the foliage. The English forests were dark and heavy in color and the trees were covered very thickly with leaves, creating deep and intense shadows underneath them. Our own countryside always strikes me as being about midway between these two extremes, more brilliantly green than either of them, and of course in the fall glaring with an intense brilliance unknown in European countries.) French children, even in the cities, seemed very quiet and well bred and were always politely interested in seeing one paint or draw, but they were never rude or boisterous like the little gnomes with whom I had had dealings at home. In fact, French people generally were so accustomed to the sight of artists working in their midst that outside of a casual scrutiny they seldom bothered one by getting in the way or making foolish remarks.

On the other hand, the Jardin des Plantes wasn't much of a zoo. It was dirty, smelly, dark and uncomfortable generally, yet there the great Frenchmen Borge[17], [Emmanuel] Fremiet[18] and several others have done most of their studies for the splendid statues of animals, unsurpassed by any work of later days. Rules and plenty of them seemed a

[17] I could not find any reference to an artist named Borge. Perhaps Knight meant Eugène Antoine Borga, an animal sculptor active in this period. More likely, though not as close in spelling, he meant Antoine Louis Barye, Fremiet's predecessor as Professor of Drawing at the Jardin des Plantes. Knight refers to Barye — by name and correctly spelled — elsewhere in his manuscript, though, so we can't be sure who he's referring to here.

[18] Emmanuel Fremiet (1824–1910) was, after Barye, the finest and best known of the French sculptors known as *Les Animaliers* and is responsible for bringing animal sculpture into fashion with the collecting world. His mother was an accomplished artist, as was his cousin Sophie, an excellent painter and early mentor to the young artist. A prodigy, Fremiet began receiving formal art training at the age of five and was accepted into the famed École des Artes Decoratifs at thirteen.

Knight was not alone in being influenced by him, as Fremiet tutored many American artists who came to Paris. He often had more than twenty students working at his studio or in the Louvre, where he was Director of Sculpture. His work, while based on detailed practical knowledge of anatomy he gained in morgues and with taxidermists, is never cold and academic. As just one example, his many versions of "Gorille enlevant une femme" give Fay Wray and King Kong a solid run for their money in terms of action and drama! For more about him, see *Emmanuel Fremiet, 1824-1910: La Main et le Multiple* by Catherine Chevillot (Dijon: Musée des beaux-arts de Dijon, 1988).

. . . Fremiet and several others have done most of their studies for the splendid statues of animals, unsurpassed by any work of later days.

prime requisite to all work in the old Garden, and those rules were certainly an awful bore, and prevented one from working and accomplishing much in the way of real study. There were pink tickets, blue tickets and yellow tickets, each for a different day, and for certain houses. Mondays one could work in the lion house, Tuesdays in the monkey houses, &c. I soon tired of the seemingly endless restrictions and henceforth confined my labors to making photos of the various creatures with a huge and cumbersome glass plate camera, foisted upon me by John Rowley just before I got on the boat. How I did work on those sensitive and many times insensitive plates, carrying the bulky machine and its accompanying tripod with me to the Zoological Garden, and standing with my head under a black cloth while I took many close-ups of iron bars with an occasional animal in the dim and often foggy distance. They cost money, those blessed plates, and were heavy as lead to carry about. When I think how I labored over those old photographs and how I lugged that huge camera about for hours in the hot sun it makes me envious of the tiny little highly efficient cameras of the present day, with their lightning fast films and powerful lenses. Photography today is a pleasure, but then it was a most arduous task, requiring actual physical strength as well as great skill and patience. Strength I had, of a sort, but as to skill and patience, they were lacking, so photography forever became a lost art for me after my Paris experiences.

⁂

The Louvre, of course, was prescribed cultural necessary number one. We did it (and it pretty nearly did us) from end to end and top to bottom, along with all the other museums in *Baedeker* — The Cluny Palace, which I loved, and the beautiful Luxembourg gallery in its lovely gardens. I vastly admired the superbly cut and modeled figures in that splendid collection of contemporary art, and it was to me (as it has been to thousands) an eye opener in the realm of matchless technique and refined taste. For in those days a man had to be a real master of his art in order to be recognized, and only the serious, intense and gifted artist could hope for recognition by a jury of his peers. There was none of the slap-dash, hideous, crude and childish stuff such as we see today exhibited all about us, and we did not have to listen to propaganda and slogans about everyone being an artist if only he cared to express himself in paint or stone.

At night we'd go to shows, sometimes opera, sometimes a little circus, riding about on the tops of the busses where the foxy conductors gave us all sorts of incongruous and worthless coppers from widely distant countries in exchange for our good French francs. Robinson, the little pleasure park near Paris, was a most bizarre and interesting spot in which to while away a few carefree hours. Huge trees grew all about and in these trees at different levels some ingenious soul had placed small platforms just large enough for a little table and four chairs, the resting places being connected by a slim and shaky ladder. Anyone who so desired could ascend this ladder and, seating himself at one of the little tables, could order what he wished from the several waiters who ran up and down the quivering steps with the agility of monkeys. Food was taken on high in a basket suspended by a rope attached to a pulley at the very top of the tree trunk. It was fun sitting in the tree top and having one's supper, and we supplemented this by blowing oddly shaped horns, sold to us by the management. All newly married poor French couples came often to this cheap little place, the girls in their frowsy white satin dresses and the grooms also in their best. They and their friends had a brief hour or two of gaiety and then they all returned to Paris where life for the poor girls would henceforth be one long grind of hard and continuous work. It was all very simple and very French in its funny little way, and we enjoyed our visits there.

❀

I feel that my praise of the point of view taken by the French masters may seem a trifle overdrawn, but I am prepared to say that in other ways the French were woefully lacking. Living, as we lived it, was cheap, but not too cheap considering what we got for it (very little) and that we were content to put up with all sorts of inconveniences which no one thought of tolerating back in the States. Plumbing was merely a name to them, and one which they could barely comprehend, to judge from the dreadful sanitary conditions of most houses in the French capital. Our little apartment did boast a toilet, but the pipe went straight down and all flushing was done from a bucket. Imagine the danger and the crudity of this installation, something unheard of in this country, where the deadly effect of sewer gas is so well recognized. Yet our apartment was new and considered up to date and the older and larger houses in which dozens of people pass their entire lives just don't have anything. Water, except bottled water, seltzer or Evian, we never drank because it forsooth wasn't considered fit to drink. Yet Paris had had years and years to remedy this shocking condition if the city authorities had seen fit to do so. The fact of the matter was that they were totally indifferent to the whole business and couldn't or wouldn't appreciate the danger.

We were young, strong, and could laugh it off, but it has always been a mystery to me how so many of our refined and delicate American maids and otherwise used to flock to Paris and live without complaining in the most sordid and atrocious surroundings — an environment that would have simply shocked them unspeakably had they been obliged to put up with it at home. To be sure, it was cheap, but not cheap at all for what one received in return: miserable beds, unhealthy dirty dark rooms, no sanitary arrangements other than what I have described, and a dingy, noisy, dirty and unhealthy neighborhood in the bargain. Maybe it was Parisian glamour, I don't know, but it was a fact, and we all knew it. Prudishness too rather petered out in France (and other parts of Europe for that matter), and our prim older ladies and elegant young ones would gaze unmoved upon sights that would have turned their heads in the States. Of course it proves what I have always maintained — that the human animal is pretty tough when it comes to standing things and can put up with an awful lot of unpleasantness and make the best of it, if necessary. Nowadays were there any Paris to go to[19] I don't believe we'd be so shocked. We are ourselves altogether broader, not to say lower, in our ideas of what is what in social behavior, and the sights we all see about us right in our own country and the conversation of our supposedly higher classes might give even a Frenchman food for thought. At any rate, in my day in Paris, Americans ignored all these things, drank their bad coffee and sour old red ink, ate occasional horse and plenty of *pâté de fois gras* and camembert and loved it. They were really philosophical about it, reasoning justly that they didn't have to go there after all, unless they so elected, and were prepared to accept whatever came along in a truly cosmopolitan spirit. It was the only way, and it was the correct one, because Paris had wonderful things to offer in the realms of higher art and science and its more sordid aspects were soon forgotten.

Antwerp

Antwerp, the wonderful old Belgian city, was quite a revelation, totally different from Paris, but equally interesting. There was a magnificent

---

[19] This section was apparently written during the occupation of France in the second World War.

zoo, in striking contrast to the Jardin des Plantes, and the old buildings along the Scheldt and the great pictures by the Dutch and Flemish masters thrilled me no end. There was a certain brusque, rude quality about Antwerp and its people that quite fascinated our youthful minds, and the clear fresh air that blew in from the sea was most invigorating. The food was excellent, much better than Paris, with delicious fish — halibut in particular a prime favorite for me.

The Plantin Museum[20], the house of an early printer, was a most fascinating place, still filled with all the tools of an ancient worker in the art of bookmaking, and the great cathedral housed several of Rubens' famous paintings, chief among them being the "Descent from the Cross." Here was Rubens at his most splendid best, the great canvasses, brilliant and glowing and as if painted yesterday something quite new to me, and the museum contained many fine examples of his smaller paintings as well. Surely the great Fleming was magnificent, and his canvasses even today are exceedingly well preserved. The superb zoological garden was

---

[20] After working as a bookbinder in Antwerp for six years, Christoffel Plantin (1520–1589) founded his publishing house, *De Gulden Passer* (The Golden Compasses) in 1555. He moved his printing business to the Vrijdagmarkt square in a building that is now the oldest part of the Plantin-Moretus Museum. Jan Moretus (1543–1610) inherited the printing firm after marrying Plantin's daughter Martina, and between the families the business continued on the same site for over two hundred more years.

Plantin is famous for printing the *Biblia Polyglotta* (Bible in five languages: Hebrew, Latin, Greek, Syriac and Aramaic) but his company's innovations in printing technology are even more remarkable. Plantin has a legitimate claim to ushering in an early Industrial Revolution via his assembly line setup, while at the same time maintaining the highest standard of craft and quality via his employment of the best type and graphic designers in the world. In 1877 the family living quarters and the printing offices opened to the public. The museum houses the two oldest surviving printing presses in the world and complete sets of punches and matrices; visitors both in Knight's day and ours experience their entire printing process, from cutting type in the letter foundry to making final corrections in the proofing rooms. You can learn more from Theodore Low De Vinne's *A Printer's Paradise: The Plantin-Moretus* (San Francisco: The Grabhorn Press, 1929).

There was a magnificent zoo . . .

a great treat for me, and I spent many hours there drawing from choice specimens of many rare species of animals not yet shown in our own country. The Garden was a private affair and had many wealthy Antwerp businessmen as patrons. There were fine restaurants, music, and charming walks and vistas in this most interesting spot. A great deal of money had been spent on the grounds and buildings which housed the various classes of animals, and all specimens were carefully and cleverly selected so as to make a good showing for exhibition purposes. The big cats had fine great cages in which to display their splendid proportions and everything was immaculate and expertly cared for by scores of trained helpers. All in all, it was a wonderfully interesting spot.

Amsterdam

Our next adventure was to be Amsterdam, the Hague and other Dutch cities. The busy Dutch town was if anything noisier and more boisterous than Antwerp, and many of the people seemed never to go to bed, rushing up and down the streets all night, singing and shouting at the top of their lungs. These Hollanders were huge eaters, too, like their Flemish neighbors, but the food, while plentiful, didn't appeal to me. There was too much pickled herring, hard boiled eggs, and cheese to suit me, and it was very expensive. The chocolate, however, was the best in the world, either for eating or drinking, and the Dutch consumed great quantities of it at all times. They were a tremendously vigorous and virile people, kindly, shrewd and able. Big, brawny and tireless, I saw in them the descendants of the stout old Burghers who had built up our own city of New York ("New Amsterdam," in earlier times) and fought and traded with the Indians in the great new country across the sea.

The Rijksmuseum was our chief focal point in Amsterdam, and thither we proceeded as soon as possible to feast our eyes upon its many

For here were shown the cream of all that had made Holland great in art . . .

artistic treasures, and indeed they were treasures, these big and little pictures by the great old masters of the Dutch School. We gazed with reverent admiration at the round and ruddy faces of long dead Burghers and their handsome, stolid wives, all beautifully drawn and painted and life-like to the last degree. For here were shown the cream of all that had made Holland great in art, superb van Eycks[21], exquisite little ter Borchs[22], realistic still lifes, and last and most wonderful of all, the magnificent Rembrandts, including the so called "Night Watch." Surely this great picture, which has stirred the enthusiasm of thousands, is well worth a trip across the ocean to see. Yet it was this very painting that by a curious streak of irony presaged the fall from grace of the finest of all Dutch painters, perhaps the greatest who ever lived in any country. For, sad to relate, his models, the members of a certain Guild, were not pleased with their portraits. Or at least some were not — those that Rembrandt had chosen to put back into the shadows in order to enhance the effect of the whole.

[21] The techniques Jan van Eyck (1390?–1441) used to create the striking realism in his paintings, most specifically "Portrait of Giovanni Arnolfini and His Wife," have become the subject of debate in recent years. In his book *Secret Knowledge: Rediscovering the Lost Techniques of the Old Masters* (NY: Viking Studio, 2001), David Hockney proposes that van Eyck and some of his contemporaries used optical means such as concave mirrors, lenses, and *camera obscura* as aids well before they became common tools. Scientific analysis ("Optics and realism in renaissance art" by David G. Stork, *Scientific American*, vol. 291, no. 6, December 2004, 76-83) calls these theories into doubt, though.

[22] Gerard ter Borch the Elder gave up an artistic career for a more financially stable profession as a tax collector, but encouraged his children to pursue the arts. His daughter Gesina was a skilled water-colorist who illustrated a number of published albums, and another son Moses excelled at portraiture. But it was Gerard ter Borch the Younger (1617-1681) who achieved the greatest fame.

Known for his intimately scaled portraits of Dutch burghers, regents, and clergymen, arguably his best works are his portrayals of quiet and contemplative scenes, particularly of women engaged in everyday tasks. In this he was a major influence on Vermeer, who got to know ter Borch personally just as he began his career. *Gerard ter Borch*, by Adriaan Waiboer and Mary Davis (NY: American Federation of Arts, 2004) provides a brief biography and reproduces some of his best — and sometimes controversial — paintings.

At any rate it was not a success as far as his clients were concerned, and as is well known poor Rembrandt died almost in want, he whose most meager scratchings bring huge prices today. And so his prestige suffered and his career forthwith began its downward course to end in poverty and oblivion. Thus did the Dutch (at the time) regard their most brilliant genius. It's a sorry story, but it has happened before and will probably happen again.

England

London I vaguely remembered as a small boy with my stepmother and father, but upon returning I took a different view of the great city. We hunted up a boarding house and like so many Americans found one in the very neighborhood of Baker Street. "Hupper Byker Street" was what our cabby called it, and it wasn't so very far from either the Zoo in Regent's Park or the British Museum, both so interesting to me. It was a big house, one of a row, and we had good rooms, and the place was clean and quiet. The Misses Guard oversaw this menage, and they were two maiden ladies well fitted for their position. I can't say they were generous when it came to meals, but at any rate what we had was good and well cooked. How one of the ladies who always did the serving could always so exactly apportion the different viands I never could quite make out, but when the last guest had been served just once there wasn't so much as a string bean left in the dish, and this dish was never replenished. A second helping was entirely out of the question. No doubt this scanty fare was sufficient to sustain life, but it didn't specially add to the gaiety of the dinner table, so to cheer our waning spirits the other Miss Guard became a sort of self-appointed joke maker and general social entertainer. She was the younger of the two, rouged heavily over her thin and prominent cheekbones, and she

The tremendous bits of glittering loveliness were kept in constant motion . . .

wore the most curious long jewelry, consisting of necklaces, bracelets, ear rings, and great breast pins of bizarre design. Strangely enough, it wasn't so very different from the kind of thing that has become the fashion of later years, but up until then I had never seen any of it. The necklaces were like strings of boxes, or a series of lockets, all in heavy gold of various shades and colors, and the bracelets were matching ornaments of the same odd shapes. The tremendous bits of glittering loveliness were kept in constant motion by the animated lady, who laughed uproariously at her own mild jokes and was evidently there for the sole purpose of giving the guests a good time and also diverting their attention from the undoubted fact that the food was exceedingly meager in quantity.

In the main, however, it was a jovial household, and I must say, the ladies with all their funny ways were always ladies, which was a great treat after the everlasting waiters and waitresses of continental dining rooms. The splendid zoo in Regents Park was all that a person of my peculiar leanings could ask for — a magnificent collection of animals, birds and reptiles from all parts of the world lived in this most elaborate garden, and to it thousands of people went daily to enjoy themselves in a quiet way, gazing at the creatures from strange lands across the sea, and taking tea at one of several restaurants scattered about the grounds. I don't remember any music as in continental zoos, but I didn't miss it, as I came for a different purpose.

Florida

The summer and early fall after my return from Europe found me in poor condition. I was nervous, and not very strong, and about Christmas time I felt very miserable. These feelings I described at length to Dr. Frank Chapman, a very early friend of mine at the Museum, and he advised a trip to Florida, in those days a pretty wild and primitive country outside of a few big towns. He told me in glowing terms of a wonderful spot at the Indian River where he had passed several months ten years before and had discovered a new species of muskrat and collected many rare specimens of birds and mammals. So infectious was his enthusiasm that I was at last persuaded to embark upon this somewhat vague adventure.

🦋

The house, Oak Lodge, I stayed at was situated four or five hundred feet back from the water, and was the usual Florida dwelling: flimsy and unpainted, set up on piles, and not very comfortable. One could hear every sound inside the house on account of the paperlike partitions between the various rooms, yet we all managed to have a fine time and learned a lot about each other's peculiarities. The household at first consisted of Mrs. Latham, her daughter "Queenie," occasionally Charlie Latham himself, a stout and charming sportsman Colonel Newton Dexter from Providence, and myself. Eventually Abbott Thayer[23], his son Gerard[24],

[23] Abbott Handerson Thayer (1849–1921), who studied under Gérôme, is best known in the art world for his images of idealized, winged women. He was a fanatic for birds, fresh air, and the natural world, and his art and studies led him to a theory of concealing coloration that was eventually put in practice in military camouflage. For more about his work and its early application, see Richard Meryman's article "A painter of angels became the father of camouflage" in *Smithsonian Magazine*, vol. 30, no. 1, April, 1999, 116 -128.

[24] Like Knight himself, Louis Agassiz Fuertes (1874–1927) exhibited an early interest in birds. Upon finding a live owl tied to the kitchen table, his parents realized their son's interest went very deep indeed. Fuertes' father, a teacher at Cornell University, took young Louis to the library to study Audubon's *Birds of America*, and his son drew birds for the rest of his life.

He once wrote "You know that I was born with the itching foot, and the sight of a map — or even a time-table — is enough to stir me all up inside." An expedition to Alaska, as well as trips with Dr. Elliot Coues (a leading ornithologist of his day) and Abbott Thayer shaped Fuertes' career and his desire to draw from life. He illustrated virtually every im-

and Louis Fuertes arrived for a month's sojourn. Our activities during these few weeks were certainly strenuous, as none of these eager and expert naturalists had ever been to Florida and everything was a revelation to them, particularly the bird life of the region. My knowledge of birds was of the sketchiest, but I was to witness in our collecting excursions through the marshes and near our camp just what it meant to really identify birds seen perhaps only for an instant as they fluttered into the concealing foliage. Warblers, and many other types of small birds swarmed at times in the trees on their migration north, and these are exceedingly difficult to see, owing to their diminutive bulk and protective coloration. I, of course, was merely an onlooker to these feats of optical gymnastics, and was perfectly contented to listen and learn whatever I could under the circumstances.

Abbott Thayer, a master of the theory of protective coloration, was right in his element, explaining to us his ideas on the subject from the newly shot specimens that were brought in. To me it was tremendously instructive, and our trips were the high spot of my Florida visit. Naturally we had our drawing materials with us, and I was intensely interested to see Abbott Thayer work and how his drawings compared with those made by Louis F. and myself. Abbott made two drawings, one of a few of the half grown birds standing around their nest and the other a nesting bird with body horizontal and head and neck drawn back and resting on the breast. Two quite different poses, but oh, how beautifully he did them — with wonderfully true and firm lines he put down the characteristic outlines of these singular birds and then shaded them to perfection, rounding the

portant American bird book of the early 20th century, and would certainly have done the same for the birds of Abyssinia (Ethiopia) if he hadn't died in an automobile accident shortly after his return from Africa. Frederick G. Marcham's book *Louis Agassiz Fuertes & the Singular Beauty of Birds: Paintings, Drawings, Letters* (NY: Harper & Row, 1971) provides an excellent introduction to a man who Knight admired as a friend and peer.

Abbott Thayer, a master of the theory of protective coloration, was right in his element . . .

grotesque forms, some light touches quickly completing two splendid studies, which for once in my life I promptly appropriated and which with still further foresight on my part I got him to sign then and there. Just how I had the nerve to do this I could never quite say, but it was a happy inspiration, and I still possess the wonderful and much prized drawings.

After two weeks we packed up all our things, now much increased by our newly acquired specimens and returned to the lodge, where we industriously put the finishing touches to our bird skins and arranged all the data about them. I hadn't done any drawing while on this trip, but I had learned a good bit about the science of protective coloration and the difficulties encountered in painting this complicated scheme of light, shade and color. Thayer had been an animal painter as a young man and knew what Fuertes and I might expect in our particular field. He was an ideal teacher, appreciative of serious work, highly skilled himself, and very original in his views on art. To be thrown as we were for several weeks in the company of such a man could not but help our budding talents and we both tried to make the best of our opportunities. How I wished in later years that I could have had several years instruction in the art of painting from this remarkable genius.

Like most geniuses, Thayer had his peculiarities, and a funny incident occurred soon after our return to Oak Lodge. Charlie Latham had a big white duck, the very last of a flock that someone had sent him from the north, and he naturally cherished this rather lonesome individual, which usually in duck fashion delighted in a bath in the creek just before retiring for the night. One evening I was in the house talking to Col. Dexter when we heard the roar of a shotgun coming from the direction of the creek. I rushed out only to meet Charlie Latham walking toward the house with a frown like a thunder cloud on his dark features. "What's the matter?" I asked. "Damn fool shot my tame duck," said Charlie between his clenched teeth, and marched into the house. In a minute more came

Abbott, hurrying after him, a bit sensitive, face lined with emotion. "I'm so sorry, Knight — Gerald and I shot Latham's duck. It was against the sunset, and it looked black to us!" Here indeed was a wonderful example of Abbott's coloration theory, but in this case it didn't work out in just the way we expected[25].

Toward the end of April our stay in Florida came to an end. Louis and I collected a few big snakes, gophers, chicken snakes, and pine snakes, put them in a box, and when we reached Jacksonville we covertly sneaked our pets aboard and set them on the floor in our stateroom. The ship didn't leave until the following morning, but about four o'clock, just at daylight, we heard a most tremendous racket in the adjoining room; thumpings, bangings about, and cries of "Snake!" echoed through the companionway. We were not interested, but later on when we had arisen and peered into our snake box, became very much so, for our prize chicken snake was gone. It was then that we had our first suspicion that the racket might have been because of our pet. This proved to have been the case, as we learned later when a casual inquiry elicited the facts. Our neighbor, a rather hard drinker, had woken early and gazing upward at the beam above his head was terrified by what he thought was a snake. Bounding from his berth, he seized a cane and began beating at the harmless creature, until our cherished reptile was quite defunct. Naturally, we kept very close-mouthed about our part in the affair, and saw to it that our remaining specimens were kept within bounds.

---

[25] Thayer's theories didn't all stand up, obviously! In his book *Concealing-Coloration in the Animal Kingdom* he asserted that all animal coloration, from peacock feathers to a baboon's rump, exists for the purpose of concealment. He argued, for instance that the red body of the flamingo helps conceal it against the Florida sunset. Just as with this duck example that Knight recounts, it's obviously not true. For more about the subject, and for Teddy Roosevelt's part in discrediting a theory taken too far, see Stephen J. Gould's article "Red wings in the sunset," reprinted in *Bully for Brontosaurus* (NY: W.W. Norton and Company, 1991).

Gabriel O'Reilly

To prepare to illustrate the article by Calmette, Knight's friends at the museum referred him to an expert who might help him...

This was Gabriel O'Reilly, without doubt one of the queerest of the many queer friends whom it has been my privilege to know.

When I first met O'Reilly he was living in a cheap lodging house in the west 20s or 30s. Two rooms were all he could afford, and one was occupied by a huge horned owl, which sat on a perch in one corner and glared and snapped his beak at me. The other room was set apart for O'Reilly and his snakes. The man himself was an extraordinary individual. Moderately tall and powerfully built, he had a small, almost bald head, set off by a huge beak-like nose, a Kaiser Wilhelm moustache and a pair of exceedingly brilliant glinting eyes, very fierce and bird-like in their expression. His manner was calm, but one sensed the tremendous energy which it concealed, and his actions were quick, stealthy and cat-like, almost sinister in their concentrated alertness. He spoke beautiful English with the slightest brogue, and his voice was charmingly modulated. Altogether a very strange combination of culture and almost savage primitiveness. No wonder he was an expert snake-catcher, and I could imagine him sneaking through the jungles almost on his hands and knees, seeking out some particular and deadly specimen for his collection. No snake, however large, poisonous or ferocious, could have had a chance with him, as he was as quick as any serpent, and a thousand

64

. . . without doubt one of the queerest of the many queer friends
whom it has been my privilege to know.

times more intelligent. Reptiles, particularly snakes were evidently his hobby. I might almost say his obsession, and to obtain them he would undergo the greatest fatigue and privation, but in all other activities he was lazy, indolent to a degree, and a terrible procrastinator, putting off from day to day his writing for *McClure's* and other magazines. Almost with tears in their eyes the various editors would beg him, "For God's sake, write... We want your articles, we'll pay spot cash for them." But, either he wouldn't or couldn't, except from direst necessity, get down to work and produce.

Strange, strange O'Reilly. I never knew his story fully, but he said he had been raised for the priesthood (he could read Latin as you and I would read English) but had backed out at the last moment and taken to the wilds, there to prosecute his singular urge as a collector of reptiles, poisonous and otherwise. Later, when he had moved to 23rd Street on the third floor of an old building, he occupied a dark and gloomy room on a court. To most people it would have seemed dreary, but he was proof against such surroundings, living, however, in momentary fear of his landlady. To circumvent this she-dragon (as he described her) we arranged for a code of knocks between us which would insure my being admitted, secretly and quietly. It was most amusing to see with what stealth and caution he would open the door a crack, one bright eye just showing, and draw me quickly inside, instantly bolting the door behind me. There he was in his undershirt and trousers, no air in the room, and on a table a huge bowl filled with cigarette stubs, all of which he carefully saved for future use of the remaining tobacco. His snakes in small glass-fronted boxes were all arranged in a half circle in front of his chair, in which he would sit for hours studying them. One day when I had given my "open sesame" as usual, I found him in a bad way. It seems that on the previous day a snake had died, and he having no other way of disposing of it, had put it in the trash basket outside his door. A short time later, shrieks from the terrified landlady brought dreadful realization of what had occurred. No doubt in dumping the basket she had also thrown out the defunct ophidian. This incident only increased her fear and dislike of him, however, and it was only with the greatest difficulty that I could persuade him to come out and have a bite of lunch with me. Even then there were difficulties as the bosom of his only white shirt was a sight to behold. We got around this, however, by my painting a nice white section just below the collar in my watercolor Chinese white, which I happened to have with me. This deplorable condition was not for lack of opportunities, as I have said. The magazines continually importuned him to write articles for them, but the mere fact that he had the orders seemed to place a sort of inhibition on his working, and day after day would go by while he accomplished nothing. Alas, Gabriel O'Reilly long ago passed from my ken, and I never knew what finally became of him. No doubt he was a bit mad, and may even be yet living somewhere in this world...

Jean-Léon Gérôme and Emmanuel Fremiet

Not long after I reached Paris and when I had made a few careful studies from living animals in the Jardin d'Acclimatation, I went to see [Jean-Léon] Gérôme[26], to whom I had a letter of introduction. I shall

[26] Jean-Léon Gérôme (1824–1904) was the son of a goldsmith, who discouraged him from taking a trial apprenticeship in a Paris art studio. He didn't thrive there and ended up painting religious cards and selling them on the steps of churches to survive. Eventually, though, Gérôme secured a commission from the French government to paint a large historical canvas, "The Age of Augustus and the Birth of Christ." He traveled extensively through Europe and Asia Minor to do research for the piece, and the money he made from it allowed him to spend several more months traveling and sketching in Egypt.

He concentrated on sculpture for the last twenty-five years of his life, and his studio became a meeting place for artists, actors, and writers. Gérôme became a respected master and a professor at the École des Beaux-Arts, noted for his wit, easy-going nature

never forget that interview, as it gave me an insight into the splendid character of this brilliant and accomplished man. Gérôme, when I entered the studio (quite near the Moulin Rouge), was seated in front of his easel, painting. He rose politely, and came forward to greet me with outstretched hands. He spoke no English, but he talked slowly and clearly in French, so I understood him well. I showed him each of my drawings in turn, and for more than an hour he sat poring over my work, looking at it most intently and criticizing very kindly a few points with which he was not pleased. Nevertheless, on the whole he was very enthusiastic, and generous in his talk, probably because he saw that I was a very serious hard worker and not a mere dabbler at the business.

He was a very handsome man, rather small, very dark, with masses of curly gray hair, a moustache and little goatee, and altogether splendid to look at as his bearing was much that of a soldier — straight and somewhat austere. As all the drawings I had seen by him had been on white paper, I was surprised to hear him advise me to work on colored paper in my studies, some tone of which would approximate the body color of the animal to be drawn, and that by a lightening with white and a darkening in pencil or crayon a very realistic effect could be secured quite simply. So we talked and chatted until I thought it time to go, he apparently being in no hurry to resume his labors, and I entranced by his presence and conversation. It was a most delightful interview and impressed me deeply. He the great French painter, whose works were in every gallery, I an unknown American artist, poor and not even in any of his classes. No doubt he thought I was English, a race he disliked, but it made no difference when it came to art, which to him apparently had no barriers. He gave me a letter to his friend

coupled with rigorous teaching methods, and his hostility to the Impressionists. His work appears in many books, including *Jean-Léon Gérôme: Monographie Révissé, Catalogue Raisonné mis à Jour* by Gerald M. Ackerman (Courbevoie : ACR, 2000).

Their words of wisdom and the way in which they were spoken
left a lasting impression on our minds . . .

Fremiet, and I bowed myself out, walking on air, as I congratulated myself on my good luck.

The next day I took Gérôme's letter to Fremiet and was received in exactly the same way. I knew his work from the Jardin des Plantes, where in one part of the garden there was a fine statue by him of a bear fighting a primitive hunter. The man had just killed her cub, which dangled by a thong from his belt, and the savage brute had her powerful forearms locked around the poor fellow as she prepared to tear him to pieces. It was a thrilling and dramatic piece of work, splendidly executed and full of life and action. Meeting him now, I was surprised to see a small, meek looking individual whose tremendously powerful work was totally at variance with his temperament and physical appearance. He was more like a professor than an artist, but he took the same interest in my work as Gérôme and gave me the same sort of fatherly advice. No wonder my heart warmed to these two celebrated men, whose time was mine, as a fellow student in the great field of animal painting and sculpture. My American friends, who worked in Paris, have always told me that they too received the same kindly criticism and encouragement from their masters, all men of world wide reputation. Their words of wisdom and the way in which they were spoken left a lasting impression on our minds at a time when such encouragement was most valuable.

Edward Drinker Cope

Professor Edward Drinker Cope[27], of the Academy of Sciences in Phila-

[27] Edward Drinker Cope (1840–1897) was one of America's first paleontologists, and his influence is still felt today. He published over a thousand scientific papers, including many on dinosaurs and many more on early mammals.

Brought up in a fairly well-to-do Quaker family, he never took to the life of a gentleman farmer that his father wanted for him. He was more interested in what was below the land than what was above it. (Not so much that he considered himself a geologist. He

delphia, was an outstanding genius in many lines of research, and for years before I met him had been a most successful collector of fossil creatures in our western country. The vast regions west of the Mississippi were very wild and woolly even in my day, but in the 70s they were decidedly dangerous collecting grounds — heat, cold, thirst, hunger, and hostile Indians were just a few of the difficulties which then beset the seeker after new and wonderful species of fossil animals.

Cope, and Marsh[28] of Yale, were practically pioneers in this field

commented that Darwin's *Voyage of the Beagle* was "exceedingly interesting, only it had too much geology in it.") His fortunes — both financial and professional — rose and fell a number of times during his lifetime. In the end, he was most famous for his huge fossil collection, his combative personality, and his feud with rival Othniel Charles Marsh.

Of one of his discoveries, he advised Henry Fairfield Osborn: "It's no use looking for the Greek derivative for *Anisouchus cophater*, because it is not of classical origin. It is derived by the union of 'Cope' and 'hater,' for I have named it in honor of the number of them who surround me." Osborn wrote the definitive biography of his friend, titled *Cope: Master Naturalist* (Princeton: Princeton University Press, 1931).

[28] Othniel Charles Marsh (1831–1899) and Cope probably never came to blows, though both Cope's biography and *O. C. Marsh: Pioneer in Paleontology* by Charles Schuchert and Clara M. LeVene (New Haven, CT: Yale University Press, 1940), give every indication that their agents may well have.

Regardless, they were enemies in a way that only two people who are very much alike can become. Marsh had two important advantages over Cope, though. First, he had more political savvy, and became the president of the American Association for the Advancement of Science (placing him in a position of power over Cope.) Second, he had a rich uncle. George Peabody, already mentioned above in relation to J. S. Morgan, told him "If I make you rich, you will never do anything." So he didn't, instead providing Marsh with the means to become both a professor at Yale and director of the new museum there. (The Peabody Museum, naturally!) Thanks to Marsh, that museum's collection rivaled that of the American Museum of Natural History. Not to imply that Marsh was not a good and influential paleontologist. He was, and we still use his names for dinosaur groups — sauropods, theropods, and ornithopods — today. And with nineteen to his credit, he remains the all-time record holder in terms of naming dinosaur genera.

For more about Cope and Marsh, see *Bone Sharps, Cowboys, and Thunder Lizards: A Tale of Edward Drinker Cope, Othniel Charles Marsh, and the Gilded Age of Paleontology* by Jim Ottaviani and Big Time Attic (Ann Arbor, MI: G.T. Labs, 2005).

(but there really had been others before them), and these two doughty individuals had discovered and brought home some truly marvelous new creatures, early mammals and dinosaurs among them. They were deadly enemies, though, and by that I mean they really did despise each other, and as neither was averse to saying and even doing some very extreme things when their cherished specimens and scientific reputation were at stake, they, I believe, on one occasion actually came to blows. It was too funny, a regular tempest in a teapot, this wrangling, fussing and fighting over some poor old horny-headed *Triceratops* or a big-legged *Brontosaurus*, but it is an actual fact that they quarreled frequently, viciously and vehemently.

I had only recently been working on an elaborate set of illustrations for the Century Co. on an article about the Corbin Estate in New Hampshire. Here, at the time, Mr. Corbin had released a number of big animals: moose, I believe, American elk, Virginia deer, European wild boars, and American bison. All these I had carefully drawn in the old Philadelphia Zoo, and they were at the time my most ambitious attempts in illustration. I had grown fond of the City of Brotherly Love, where indeed I was very kindly treated, and so was delighted when I learned that I might have other things to paint there. I learned through the Century Co., that a certain Dr. Ballow[29] had written an article on prehistoric reptiles under Prof. Cope's direction and that Ballow wished me to illustrate it.

Forthwith, I journeyed to the big town, secured a room in a cheap boarding house, and the next day I made my first visit at Professor Cope's

---

[29] This is the one misspelling I've left as is, since it's reasonable to assume that Knight never knew this man's real name. "Dr." William Hosea Ballou might have forgotten it himself at times, since he was so used to creating fictional details about his life. He was a faker, in other words, and just about all the credentials listed in his *Who's Who* entry, from his imaginary Ph.D. on down to the date and place of birth, are suspect. This doesn't bode well for the accuracy of his scientific reporting, which included an infamous series of stories in the *New York Herald* about the feud between Cope and Marsh.

house. He lived at 2102 Pine Street (I shall never forget the number) and the dwelling itself was commonplace enough, being one of those small red brick houses with a single white marble step that one sees by thousands in old Philadelphia. Inside everything was unique and completely dust covered. Never have I seen such a curious place — just like the kind that Dickens would have loved. Piles of pamphlets rose from floor to ceiling in every narrow hallway, leaving just enough room to squeeze by them and no more. At the right as I entered, I looked into the front parlor. Shuttered with inside blinds, the floor was completely hidden by the massive bones of some vast creature, probably a dinosaur. Dust lay thick here as elsewhere, and the place was absolutely bare of furniture and hangings. No pictures, no curtains, nothing but the petrified skeletons of extinct monsters more or less carefully disposed in every available open space. This in itself was peculiar but it merely introduced one to the strange sights to be encountered in this almost sinister domicile. The second floor, to which I was promptly conducted, was reached by a narrow stair, the wall side of which carried small shelves holding pickled snakes and other reptiles in bottles. The back room on this floor was a long, narrow affair with a bay window overlooking a meager garden. This room, sacred to all good Philadelphians as a sitting room or back parlor, was one of the most singular places I have ever seen. It, too, was littered with various objects from end to end, all piled helter skelter on tables, chairs and shelves. A human skull grinned at me from the mantle, and a large bronze vulture spread its menacing pinions above a cage containing a live Gila monster. Bones, recent and fossil, were everywhere, all dusty, and all in apparently inextricable confusion. But Cope himself, the presiding genius among all this scientific chaos, met me with a genial and charming smile, made me sit down and talked, as only Cope could talk, about the things I came to discuss.

So began a most interesting acquaintance with this wonderful man

So began a most interesting acquaintance with this wonderful man . . .

whose physical powers, alas, were even then on the wane, owing to a deadly disease which was soon to progress to its fatal conclusion. I did not realize this at first, but Cope in a few days quite casually told me of his serious condition, not seeming in the least perturbed, though admitting that he did not feel particularly strong or well. However, we were soon engrossed in our subject. I was given a drawing table in the bay window (the only free space in the room) and there every day for the ensuing two weeks I listened with rapt attention to the greatest conversationalist that ever graced the service of Paleontology. With matchless charm this brilliant mind presented the difficult subject to me. He was a tyro in the field. Under the spell of his facile tongue new vistas of the life of the past opened before me in a way I had never dreamed of, and Cope drew pictures for me, pictures of the creatures I had to do for the magazine, and many others, and explained with delightful clarity the methods by which he had arrived at certain conclusions regarding the forms and proportions of these monsters. Under his expert guidance I felt that I had stepped back into an ancient world — filled with all sorts of bizarre and curious things, and in imagination I could picture quite distinctly just what these mighty beasts looked like as they walked or swam in search of food. It was only natural therefore that I applied myself most energetically to the making of my little sketches, took notes, and got Cope's approval of them, enjoying myself hugely meanwhile in such inspiring company.

As the days went by, I got to know the master better. He talked and I listened while he rapidly went over the whole subject of paleontology and its connection with the life of the present day. For with Cope as with Osborn, this intense study of the ancient in connection with the modern was an outstanding characteristic of all their work in science. For here was no mere investigator of dry bones, but a true genius who applied his profound knowledge of the life of the present to a clarification and explanation of the life of the past. His family affairs were always a trifle vague, but I gleaned that while he had a wife and daughter at Haverford he lived here practically alone, with the exception of a stenographer (who came every day and wrote his letters and arranged his papers) and a couple of male assistants who prepared his fossil specimens and supposedly cleaned up the place. His bedroom at the front of the house and on the same floor where I worked was also a strange and uncanny spot. Again the pamphlets made a wall from floor to ceiling, completely concealing his little cot from the hallway and leaving only a tiny space about the bed with room for one chair. Here, when Cope was too ill to rise, he would dictate to his stenographer his notes and articles. The preparators' laboratory, if we might call it so, was on the third floor back, a small room lighted by windows and a skylight. Here, old Geismer, his faithful German helper, worked hard hour after hour scraping, piecing and setting up the various bones and skeletons which Cope had collected in his travels. At the time of my visit, he was working on a wonderfully rare and primitive creature, *Phenacodus*, an Eocene fossil of a peculiar nondescript type and practically unique in its completeness. This animal, looking at first glance something like a cross between a leopard and a tapir if one can imagine such a thing, was to be mounted as found, one side only relieved of the overlying matrix.

Thus the little house in Pine Street grew into my life, a strange place filled with strange things, but forever associated in my mind with the brilliant scientist who presided over its treasures, and by his genius made them live again to startle and profoundly interest an astonished world. I was exceedingly lucky to have gone there just when I did because in a few months Professor Cope passed away, leaving behind him a vast accumulation of treasures, a splendid collection of rare fossils and the impress of his virile and extraordinary personality. Professor Osborn and myself felt that we should attend his funeral, and made the trip to Haverford to the house of Cope's relatives where he lay at rest before his final interment. Again the atmosphere surrounding him was unique for Cope, who having been born a Quaker was a very poor one himself and scoffed at and made all manner of fun of these good, kindly and upright people. Now they surrounded his earthly clay on every side, but even in death he still seemed to mock them. There was a profound silence as Professor O. and I entered the room, silence of the kind that hurts, but no one could think of anything to say about the man who now was lying here so still and peaceful. It was awful, and we sat with bowed heads for what seemed an interminable time, listening in vain for the spirit to move some good Quaker friend to say a few kind words over the body of the departed. This proved almost an impossibility, however, and we were just at the point of breaking when some worthy individual struggled to his feet, hastily mumbled a few blurred sentences, the service was over, and the great anatomist was now carried to his last resting place. His reputation as a scientist was secure, but his future not so secure, at least in the minds of this devout family and friends. Thus we lost Professor Cope, but I as a young and unknown man had been so fortunate as to intercept, for a time, his progress on the road to eternity.

Charles R. Knight, 1899

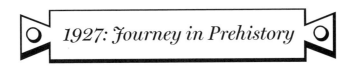

1927: Journey in Prehistory

With the 19th century drawing to a close, his work with Cope ended, and his travels abroad complete for the time being, Knight began his career in earnest. But one last section of his autobiography remains: It ties together all of the previous sections as Knight, now a world famous animal (both past and present) artist, returned to France with his family, and in the company of a few more remarkable colleagues.

In the Summer of 1927 my wife, daughter and myself went to visit some of the Prehistoric Caves of France and Spain with Henry Field, then an anthropologist at the Field Museum of Natural History in Chicago[30], and our mentor and guide in this truly wonderful adventure: Abbé Henri Breuil, celebrated savant from the Collège de France and world expert on the art and general culture of prehistoric man[31].

[30] The Field Museum of Natural History was not named after Henry Field (1902–1986), but he did have a significant influence on its development, first as assistant curator for physical anthropology and then as its Curator from 1934–1941. In 1941, President Franklin D. Roosevelt asked him to join his staff as anthropologist and personal advisor. Field became a member of the White House's Special Intelligence Unit, and director of the "M" project, a study of world population, migration and settlement used to shape post-war relocation strategies.

[31] Abbé Henri Breuil (1877–1961) trained as a priest, but made his mark on the world as a pioneer in the study of cave art. His book *Quatre Cents Socles d'Art Parietal* or *Four Hundred Centuries of Cave Art* (Montignac, Centre d'Études et de Documentation Prehistoriques, 1952) described in often romantic detail the artwork found in what he called "The Six Giants": Spain's Altamira, and France's Lascaux, Niaux, Les Trois-Frères, and Font-de-Gaume and Les Combarelles in the Dordogne, which he discovered. Alan Brodrick's book *Father of Prehistory; The Abbé Henri Breuil, His Life and Times* (NY: Morrow, 1963) gives an overview of his life.

The Abbé was a short, dark, almost bald man with brilliant full eyes, an ingratiating smile and a free but still courtly manner. A Catholic priest, but not now dressed in his formal attire, he wore for the nonce a somewhat dilapidated suit of khaki clothes, trousers tucked into leather leggings, finishing off the outfit with a pair of stout muddy shoes. He was a cultivated gentleman, a keen and mischievous host, and a mine of knowledge on many subjects, but especially on the history of men and animals of a bygone day. It was our good fortune to be thus associated with one of the very ablest men on this subject, not only because of his genial and interesting personality, but also for the reason that he had previously visited all the caves which we were to examine, and had faithfully copied many of the drawings and paintings which they contained. Thus, he was not only able to show us the pictures, but also to call our attention to the finer points in the construction of the creatures whose strange and fascinating forms we were later to gaze upon with wonder and astonishment.

Our plan was that all of us should meet at Les Eyzies, a tiny hamlet in Southern France not far from the rail-station of Perigueux on the Paris-Lyons-Mediterranean route to the Riviera. The Dordogne region in which Les Eyzies lies is world-famous for its many caves, the former homes of a host of prehistoric peoples who have left there not only great quantities of interesting implements and works of art, but also a number of actual skeletons, more or less complete, of two early races of man, the Neanderthal and Cro-Magnon types.

Henry Field, good angel of our trip, met us there and we walked across the deserted little plaza near the R. R. to a restaurant of sorts. After supper, a walk was in order along the single village street, a narrow and badly kept roadway, running almost at the foot of great cliffs which rose in sharp dark silhouette against the brilliant orb of the moon. Just above the road and right against the mighty wall, tiny houses were visible, indicated by little glowing spots of light, and with smoke coming out of the round low chimneypots. We had never before seen houses built directly against the cliff face, the near wall being the rock itself, but during our stay in this strange region we were to come upon all sorts of new and unusual sights, both natural and man-made. It was a place where the ancient world seemed not so very far removed. The air, now that the night was fully upon us grew stifling with the approach of a tremendous thunder shower, accompanied by a drenching but temporary down-pour. It was a fitting introduction to a world of life now evidenced only by the drawings and skeletal remains of the men and animals of another day. But a sky of brightest blue greeted us as we awoke the following morning after a not too peaceful night. What with the rain, the heat, the thunder and lightning, and a most vociferous rooster just under our window, there was room for improvement in our sleeping conditions. I complained about the rooster, only to learn later to my sorrow that a too-anxious-to-please host had disposed of the poor bird, to conciliate me, a nervous patron.

The Abbé had made sure that we were to lose no time seeing one of the caves. Never have I known a more restless, dynamic personality than he proved to be, a sort of caged scientific lion pacing to and fro when balked or thwarted in any way, a tremendous doer and a most persistent and energetic worker. After breakfast we were bustled into waiting cars, much in need of good springs, and off we went on our first tour of cave-inspection. The ride was short, and as we turned an abrupt corner in the road, just before us rose the majestic battlement which houses the well-known grotto of the Font-de-Gaume, most popularized and best-known of all the great group of caverns in France and Spain, containing (among many other drawings) the frieze of the woolly mammoths. This then was our first glimpse of a scene upon which, under much sterner climatic conditions, the eyes of many generations of prehistoric man had once rested. Here in very early days, the sturdy Neanderthal race had battled with some great cave-bear or pursued the herds of reindeer and bison and horses which swarmed thickly in the valleys. After them had come prehistoric artists of the Cro-Magnon race, with their chalks and gravers and little camps, to make the wonderful series of drawings which we were now to see for the first time in person. The walk to the cave was not at all difficult; a narrow but well-marked path led close under the huge rocks towering above us until we reached two oval holes in the cliff side.

It was a really dramatic moment, only possible when staged by a member of the Latin race, but we had been prepared beforehand by Henry Field as to the Abbé's very often distinctly humorous, not to say spicy, descriptions of the animals depicted so faithfully and lovingly by the ancient cave artists. At the time of their actual doing these caves existed in a state of complete and absolute blackness until broken by the fitful light of the tiny lamps carried by the Cro-Magnon masters. But nowadays these same walls reflect the light from strings of small electric globes suspended above them. We had come far to see these productions and now we gazed with unalloyed pleasure and astonishment at the long series of mammoths, bison, horses, reindeer, and other creatures now long extinct. The woolly mammoths all in a line, head to tail, and with their great recurving tusks and high foreheads, gave one a distinct feeling of awe and admiration for the skill of the man who had painted and incised their curious outlines thousands of years ago. What had he thought as he laboriously cut those forms with a piece of flint into the softer substance of the cave wall? Was it for mere pleasure that he had so inscribed them or was he giving vent to a fervent wish for better hunting and immortalizing his wishes at the same time? We shall never know...

...but now the Abbé is talking in his broken yet fluent English, pointing out with his cane the special outlines of the mammoths, superimposed upon earlier drawings of bison, horses, and reindeer. We listen carefully — it is our first lesson in prehistory. "You see," he is saying, "Zee hye — Zee nois — Zee maus — Zee tronc — Zee défenses — (pardon) — Zee tusks — Zee great igh ead and ump or zee back — Zee tail, so short — Zee bully — Zee hin quartier." This latter word stumped us all for a moment (I dared not look at Henry Field, grinning in the background), but soon it was clear: hind quarters, of course, and a favorite expression of the Abbé's who I think was very proud of the way in which he pronounced the difficult word.

So it went from animal to animal. The mammoths, reddish in color and carved with their long drooping hair, came first but the others, bison, etc. received careful attention. As we moved slowly towards the back of the long, narrow crevice, I noted with wonder the very uneven wall surfaces and found it hard to imagine anyone selecting such a spot for drawing a long series of mammoth images.

The bison was to me, as an animal painter, especially interesting. This was, of course, the European bison or wisent, an animal now practically extinct in Europe, and a taller and more ponderous creature than our own. The horses, too, with their upright manes and scrubby tails, reminded one of the modern Przewalski types from Turkestan. Today they are extinct in this region, as are the great hairy mammoths. These latter creatures were to me intensely romantic, for I pictured in my mind's eye the artist, breaking off in the midst of his work and running to the cave entrance from which point of view he could see in the valley at his very feet the actual living specimens of the great brutes as they fed and wandered over the hard and frozen ground; trumpeting, playing, fighting, an inspiration for a personality now buried forever in the mists of time. Had I been there I too might have seen them, a thought which almost took my breath away.

A sharp exclamation from the Abbé brought me back to reality, but

We listen carefully — it is our first lesson in prehistory.

it was a totally blacked-out reality, for the simple reason that the electric lights had suddenly gone out and there we all stood petrified and in total darkness! There was no danger, because the path to the entrance was almost straight and the cave is comparatively small, but the sensation was an eerie one, and conjured up more strange fancies in my mind. Who was this man, warm breathing, who stood so close to me in the Stygian gloom? Could the artist have come back to welcome us...perhaps he'd been there all the time, and when the lights came on again we'd see him standing there in our midst, tall and naked and magnificent with his bone palette in his left hand and the sharp flint graver held firmly in the other fist?

The lights went on, and there were no people present other than our own little company, subdued and perhaps chastened by a glimpse into another world of life. The Abbé was talking and telling me that if I were to go to the back of the cave and climb the little iron ladder I would see something that I would never forget, as there was a drawing upon that wall much finer than all the others and done by some other person, a painting in fact of a woolly rhinoceros, clear, strong and beautifully executed, a *tour de force*, in fact, and I must see it. Back I went, of course, climbed the iron steps and then I saw it, quite close to my head, sharply indicated and filled with life and animation. Correctly outlined too — the long low body and short legs, the hanging hair and little tail, and the curious hump, just at the back of the long head which, armed with its two sharp and boldly outlined horns, completed one of the very finest drawings in all the world of prehistoric art. It was a revelation, and as I rejoined the party I thanked the Abbé warmly for his special interest in my work as an animal painter. I found him like that always: keen, brilliant, an artist himself of no mean ability with a sureness of line and a power to see and put down the salient points in his translation of the animal cave drawings and paintings for which he is so justly famous[32].

[32] The Abbé's interpretations of cave paintings and other prehistoric finds were controver-

There are many other cave and rock shelters in the vicinity of Les Eyzies, not all with drawings or paintings of interest, but still most valuable for a study of man's sojourn here. Le Moustier, once occupied by people of the long extinct and primitive Neanderthal race, was especially notable because of its situation on the highest of three terraces rising from the junction of two wide and shallow valleys. As a vantage point for these crude but stockily built savages it possessed great possibilities for long distance observation. Some years ago skeletal remains and implements of these ancient people were discovered near the base of the first terrace, but today the topmost cave holds far more interest for the layman. We easily climbed the gradual ascent from the valley floor to the highest terrace, and there at the very corner of the sharply angled ledge lies the shallow grotto itself. The rock surface inside the shelter (it is hardly more than that) gives the impression of having been bored out by some great auger, the concentric planes of stony soil decreasing gradually almost to a point in the center of the cavern wall. There is nothing of interest in the cave itself, but the view from the entrance is really superb, one's gaze traveling across two valleys to the hills beyond. In Neanderthal days this view would not have been quite the same as present, because of a great difference in the local climatic conditions which then were severe, with much snow and rushing ice-filled rivers roaring by the meager little shelter. Again I dreamed as we gazed across the now placid and verdant landscape, a dream of days when cave-bears and mammoths,

sial in that many saw them as *over*-interpretations. But his errors, as compelling in their own way as Knight's correct insights on the same subjects, live on in the popular imagination even as new research provides us with a more accurate but still evolving picture of our earliest ancestors.

reindeer and horses, and herds of bison and woolly rhino might have been seen grazing or wading about in the icy currents of the river...and there would be life in the grotto behind me, men chipping their pieces of flint into the great *coup de poing* or hand axes of the day, and women with their children devouring great pieces of roasted horse flesh while they fought and bickered over some small treasure, perhaps a brightly colored piece of stone or shell with which to adorn their ugly persons. Life for the Neanderthal people had few diversions — eating, drinking, fighting, hunting, weapons-making and at last oblivion. The absolute necessities only composed their earthly existence.

The Abbé's insistent voice ("Vite — Vite!") and his tapping cane telling us that it was time to return to our hotel for dinner broke my gloomy reverie in short order. Indeed food and plenty of it was (I hardly dare say it) never too far from the Abbé's thoughts, and it required an event or discovery of major importance to distract his attention from the hunger-call so well developed in him. He wasn't alone in worthy concentration upon the flesh-pots, for we all soon developed rather alarmingly good appetites under the constant physical and mental activity. But dinner, I regret to say, was not all that the word implies. Food, such as it was, seemed to be quite abundant but there was also a certain sameness in the menus from day to day. In clear weather we sat out of doors, and thin, watery soup (potage, tasting vaguely of chicken, with large chunks of bread floating about on its glistening, greasy surface) in the usual large tureens was a prominent feature in these little banquets, along with veal and string beans, and bread. As for beverages there was wine, of course, cheap red and sour as usual, water (a mild bottle of supposedly uncontaminated liquid known as Evian), and coffee, much the worse for a bath in chicory, no tea, and a pale whitish fluid, *du lait*. And always bread, which came in large circular loaves and was cut individually at the table by placing the ponderous object close against the breast and slicing towards one's anatomy with a long sharp knife. When as often happened this unwieldy portion of the staff of life fell to the ground, it was promptly retrieved. A few chicken feathers and other membranes were removed from its surface and the operation imperturbably continued.

After midday dinner we would rest for a short time, unless the irrepressible Abbé had planned some special trip which might take several hours to accomplish, in which case there would be hurried calls and frantic dressing as we swarmed into our outer garments and climbed into the waiting cars. Today it might be a trip to some old and interesting town, such as Sarlat, ancient, dirty and different, redolent with unpleasant odors, but reminiscent of the old days of French Kings, armored knights, and lovely ladies. On other occasions we visited Bugue, a modern and still dirtier town where there was nothing of special interest to see except how the other half of the French people live. Then there was La Roque Gageac, quaint, intensely strange and like something out of this world, with its tiny houses and streets jumbled closely together on the steep river bank.

Les Eyzies has so many treasures and points of interest in its own little circle of antiquities that we lived in a kind of dizzy whirl of strangely intriguing and most informative trips here and there to special places which showed evidences of early occupancy of man. But most French people apparently have never heard of it, or if they have it bears no interest for them. For the scientists, of course, this situation is genuinely welcomed because it leaves them free to pursue their research in peace and without fear of distraction. Our party, gay and noisy, descended often like a bombshell upon these usually quiet centers of ancient culture, always with the Abbé, sprightly, unconventional, intense and vociferous, to show us everything — where the various layers of soil might be disclosed in a cutting at the base of one of the rock shelters and how experts carefully digging for and uncovering various accumulations of earth and bones and implements could read, as from the pages of a book, the successive life stories of men and animals who had once occupied the sites. Many of the more valuable and informative of these objects now reposed in the charming little Museum of Antiquities, perched on a rocky shelf above the street at Les Eyzies. Here, M. [Denis] Peyrony, curator of the sanctuary, had been instrumental in forming splendid collections of objects belonging to and made by ancient man. Flints, hand-axes, scrapers, gravers, and crude stone spear heads beside images of animals in bone or ivory were all carefully labeled and exhibited to the best advantage. The local ancient history was thus very well demonstrated, especially when the active and well-informed curator himself gave us the pleasure of his personal guidance. While looking over these little examples of man's handiwork in the days of his earlier existence as a veritable human type, we must remember that at least two cultures were represented by these various objects. The crude and more roughly made artifacts of the very old Neanderthal people, as well as the more refined bone and ivory and stone implements later produced by the Cro-Magnon race whose splendid drawings I have just described. Mr. Peyrony himself, presiding genius of the Les Eyzies region, was a man of a quiet though forceful personality who actually was living at the time of our visit in a little house built close against and almost under the projecting curves of one of the great rock shelters. Why he preferred this ancient style of domicile I cannot say, because it is hard to conceive of a less desirable home site. Perhaps he wished to experience the difficulties under which his peasant neighbors had struggled for centuries, or (and more likely) there was a certain ascetic satisfaction in submitting himself to such rigors. At any rate, there he was to be found when at home, he and his good wife, urbane, strictly austere in his menage, charming and hospitable and more than anxious to meet and entertain the Abbé's protégés with very illuminating little talks on the life of his contemporaries in this small, remote and very constricted community. In his youth, he said, there was only a central fire in the village, and he was often obliged to carry burning embers to his father's home, then to cook the frugal meals whenever necessary. One's sojourn in this little place was thus at least in retrospect a partial return to a type of living which we in the States have not experienced for perhaps a hundred years.

❀

So far we had not seen, with the exception of some small pieces done in ivory or bone, any attempts at sculptures or carving, but now we learned that at a spot called Cap Blanc there was a whole frieze (six in number) of splendidly modeled horses, about one-half life size and quite unique in every way. This proved to be a truly remarkable bit of prehistoric carving in high relief. The animals, spread along a wall of soft rock for a distance of thirty or forty feet, were exceedingly well done and showed furthermore a type of horse nearly comparable to the present wild horses of Turkestan (*Equus przewalski*). My painting of three of these animals is done directly from the actual frieze and is not retouched or improved in anyway. The remarkably accurate silhouettes, showing the proportions and general contours of the animals are full of life and required an expert to execute. The curious upright mane, no forelock, and somewhat ratty tail of the modern Turkestan species is practically duplicated in these ancient sculptures, the finest things of their kind known to anthropologists. Very fortunately, the whole line of animals was apparently covered for a long period by debris falling from the top of the cliff front, with the result that the delicately cut images were saved from weathering of any kind, and to this we may ascribe their almost perfect preservation after the lapse of thousands of years. When first uncovered, a man's skeleton (possibly that of the artist who so cleverly produced these fine examples of late Cro-Magnon art) was found lying at the foot of the cliff just below the horse frieze. How he came to be there (as it did not look like an actual burial) will always remain a mystery, but there was romance in this find, the association of a work of art with a being contemporaneous with its production, one who had seen the sprightly little pony-like creatures in the flesh, as they pranced and snorted, wheeled and galloped madly in an exuberance of animal spirits perhaps 10,000 years before our day. Such excellent examples of the work of ancient artists are really an inspiration to those of us who essay to follow in their footsteps, and one feels a fraternal emotion in the presence not only of the art itself but in the meager remains of its possible producer.

It was a country for dreamy reverie, a closing of one's eyes and the envisioning of this old time life now so long passed away, but in the vicinity of the Abbé Breuil no such type of even partial somnolence could exist for more than an hour or two. "Vite — vite!", a tapping cane and a stamping impatient foot broke rudely into these vaporizings as this dynamic son of the Church planned our days here and made arrangements for our visit to other and more distant fields of explorations.

As one of the objects of our trip was the inspection and purchase by Henry Field of prehistoric remains, both human and man-made, for later exhibition in the Field Museum in Chicago, we were more or less constrained to visit certain individuals known to the Abbé as possessing desirable collections for such an exhibit. But while we remained in Les Eyzies, our hurried round of cave exploration never stopped except when darkness fell. The Combarelles Cavern, a most remarkably long and very narrow cave was known to contain scores of interesting drawings along its 700-foot walls. Numerous species not represented in the Font-de-Gaume grotto are here and as many as 400 drawings comprising an almost complete collection of the mammals of the times are represented. Lions, wolves, cave bears, reindeer, bison, stag, ibex, rhinoceros, and several crude renderings of the human form are inscribed here and there upon the stony surfaces. Though not personally observed by the writer, the tracings made by the industrious Abbé do not reveal any unusual artistic ability; that is, they cannot compare in accuracy with the rhinoceros of Font-de-Gaume, nor of many others elsewhere. Naturally, however, they are all of intense interest, because every scrap of work of this far-off period must be of vital importance to the scientist, who is thereby enabled to see for himself a more or less comprehensive exhibit of the fauna existing contemporaneously with the human beings of the last great glacial era.

※

"It's time," proclaims our mentor, "Time to be off to the great cave of Altamira in Northern Spain." So the Abbé shepherded his little flock, talking and gesticulating with splendid fervor, always desirous of preparing us for at least some of the wonders that lay ahead in order that we amateurs would not be unduly confused by the quick succession of places, scenery, and altered living conditions which he knew could be pretty difficult at times. Naturally his Spartan spirit and sinewy physique would be more than equal to what must have seemed to him merely a pleasant little holiday, announcing that we would take up our residence in the little village of Santillana quite close to the great cave we had come so far to see. We were to have rooms in a newly opened, but expensive, little hotel which was as a matter of fact an old stone private house formerly with others in the place, or a deluxe hunting lodge or domicile for rich grandees of the Royal entourage of Spain. The bedrooms surrounding a great salon on the second floor of the hostelry were spacious and high and fairly comfortable. Sanitary arrangements in spite of the newness of the place as a guest house were as usual of the scantiest and water always at a premium. One always wonders at the scarcity of water in European dwellings, especially when in most places there is such an awful lot of it outside. We were however blessed with clear weather and for several nights a magnificent moon, shining with fierce intensity, created the most wonderful illusions of light and shade in the streets of this very ancient town. At such times, as one stood at the open window and gazed across the roofs of the little village, one's imagination easily pictured the life and times of another day, more especially when a band of male singers wandering about through the streets in the moonlight gave us all a treat as we listened entranced to singing which surpassed anything we had heard on the operatic stage. The magnificent, natural voices rose in perfect harmony through the mazes of the narrow lanes and the illusion they created of a complete and realistically staged ensemble was dramatic in the extreme. Sleep during the hours of darkness seems entirely forgotten in Spain, as even the peasants apparently never went to bed except at noon for a short siesta. We could hear plainly all about us the chatter and laughter of the peasant children as they gamboled about in the moonlight to the accompaniment of guitars and concertinas played by the old folks.

Our primary object here, of course, was the inspection of the grotto of Altamira. So bright and early on our second morning we were off on our journey. It really was quite near, and very easy of access, in fact merely at the top of a rising gradient a quarter of a mile from the road. The country was barren, dry and brown, and quite treeless, with squat and squalid but extremely picturesque stone and stucco farm houses at frequent intervals, and goats, a few cattle, and donkeys grazing or wandering aimlessly about. Altamira, famed as one of the very greatest show places of prehistoric art is with other caves and grottos under the supervision of the Spanish government, and we were fortunate in meeting Dr. Obermaier, a German priest who was in charge of all such natural wonders throughout the country[33]. The doctor had hurried up from Madrid on the advent of our coming, principally to see his old time friend and confrere, the Abbé Breuil, with whom in happier times he had been closely associated in a scientific way. He proved to be a most genial host and did everything in his power to make our trip comfortable. A certain Count de la Vega, also deeply interested in the subject of prehistory, was our luncheon host on this memorable occasion, and it was most illuminating to us as Americans to see the almost feudal ceremony which prevailed during even this little repast. To make matters still more monarchistic we were honored by a visit from the Duke of Alba, royal head of all archaeological and historical monuments in Spain. As the Earl of Berwick in England and heir to numerous other high and important titles, this celebrated gentleman gave color and authority to the visit of our little party, and we felt that in Spain, at least in 1927, the monarchy stood on very firm and popular ground. How soon this illusion was to be rudely dispelled, the King (Alfonso and his English queen) deposed and even the great Duke of Alba's palace and possessions subjected to the despoiling influences of a revolutionary regime under Franco, people's champion and dictator. Extraordinary!

---

[33] Dr. Hugo Obermaier (1877–1946) was, together with Abbé Henri Breuil, the co-chair at the newly founded Institut de Paléontologie Humaine of Paris in 1911. (Like Breuil he was also ordained as a priest, though a secular one.) Taken unawares by the beginning of the First World War while working in Spain, and unable to return to Paris because he was German, Obermaier stayed there and eventually became chair of human prehistory and an associate professor at the Universidad Central in Madrid. In 1936 war — in this case the Spanish Civil War — surprised Obermaier again, this time trapping him in Norway. In 1939, despite efforts of powerful friends like the Duke of Alba, Obermaier decided to accept a professorship in Switzerland and not to return to Spain. Today, the Hugo Obermaier Society convenes in his honor.

But the cave and its treasures awaited us, and though we had been told by the Abbé that the work was of the finest, I for one was still tremendously impressed by the wonderfully outlined and richly tinted bodies of the bison herd which romps so gaily over the vast almost flat ceiling of the grotto. In 1879 or 1880 when the cavern was first examined, this ceiling came down very nearly to the floor, so close I believe that one could not stand upright in the narrow space between the two surfaces. Today a ditch has been dug running around the base of the side walls and the whole lighted by electricity, so that while its first appearance has been altered one is now enabled to see clearly and admire these truly magnificent paintings. The figures are quite large, possibly half-life size, and number about seventeen individuals of the bison species in various animated poses, two wild boars, a horse or two and a female deer. At intervals large oval bosses of stone-like flattened pillows hung from the ceiling and on these restricted areas the Cro-Magnon master had displayed some of his best talent, indicating with skill and ingenuity several of the great beasts lying down in attitudes characteristic of all cattle the world over. The paintings are amazingly spirited; bright and fresh in their tints of brown, red, black, yellow and white, the shadings beautifully accomplished and all done with a consummate ease and assurance hard to describe. They give the impression of being tossed off in the fever heat of creational stress, but with the essentials of proportion, silhouette, varied pose, and color suggestion all controlled by a perfectly competent eye and an accurate and clever hand. In other words, a splendid piece of art fashioned under the most difficult and painfully restricted conditions. The cramped and awkward position made necessary by the close approximation of the floor to the ceiling on which the work is executed would greatly deter bold and vigorous outlines. Combined with this was the always meager lighting made possible by only a tiny stone lamp and a vast hard and necessarily uneven background. However in this case the artist was superior to his medium and environment and put down by far the finest and grandest of all the artistic works of early man thus far discovered[34].

(The romantic history of this find, briefly: The Spanish savant [Marcelino Sanz de] Sautuola and his daughter were one day looking as usual for weapons and other utensils on the rough floor of the cave when the child, looking upward suddenly, called the scientist's attention to some drawings just over their heads on the low ceiling. "Oh, papa, look at the bulls" was her classic way of summing up what she saw, but strangely enough the man was not especially interested in the revelation of this great artistic treasure, so for years the extraordinary find received but scant attention from the archaeological scientists. At one time indeed the whole superb work was threatened by the blasting of some rock just above the ceiling of the grotto, explosions which might have totally destroyed this magnificent relic in its entirety. Fortunately, except for a crack in the stone (since repaired) no damage was done, thus preserving for posterity one of the grandest examples of Cro-Magnon art.)

We lingered about this enchanted region for some days, loathe to leave its many bizarre and little known points of interest. I busied myself from morning until night painting some charming little scenes, a rustic farm house, the old and rare Romanesque cathedral in the town itself, and an inner courtyard of an old house, where a tiny black donkey standing beneath a ruined stone arch of great antiquity gave a touch of life to an otherwise somnolent bit of ancient Spanish domain. The streets and the people were wonderful, the children little devils incarnate and mis-

[34] Imagine what Knight would have made of the Chauvet caves, discovered in the 1990s! The skill evident in the paintings found there (it seems clear that the artists had had specific training) coupled with evidence of religious practices dating back tens of thousands of years, would have thrilled him. See *Dawn of Art: The Chauvet Cave, the Oldest Known Paintings in the World* by Jean-Marie Chauvet (NY: H.N. Abrams, 1996) for both beautiful images and for a reminder that we still have much to discover, much to learn.

chievous as a pack of baboons. Every time they saw me emerge from the hotel with my easel and canvas they would scream like miniature furies "Pinter, pinter!" and gathering around me in a tight and smelly circle would begin to perform impudent monkey tricks to my irritation and trepidation. They stuck their dirty fingers into the soft paint of the palette, made faces at me, stood in my way, assumed more or less indecent attitudes and conducted themselves generally like the little hoodlums they were. I didn't dare to slap any of them for fear of reprisals from the old folks who strangely enough paid not the slightest attention either to me or my picture, something very unusual in street painting in other countries, where as a rule, one is a perfect mecca of interest from the first stroke of the brush. Chocolate — sweet, sticky and cheap — saved the day here for me, my good wife purchasing it in large cakes at a nearby shop, and feeding bits of the dark brown oozy substance to each little urchin in turn with the result that in a few days no longer was I insulted, browbeaten, and laughed at, but on the contrary my advent became almost a reverent gathering place for the infant life of the neighborhood, and when a canvas was completed and I rose to go, sweet smiles, gentle good wishes and positive tears of regret for the end of the chocolate dispensation became the order of the day. It was a difficult departure in fact, because on sober reflection, these poor little aimless waifs were growing up in an atmosphere of real destitution and privation. What happened to them in the terrible years that followed one does not care to contemplate. It was a phase of life which with its poverty and meager living conditions contrasted strangely with that of the ladies and gentlemen who came nightly to our hotel from nearby Santander, the big part of the Bay of Biscay. These refined and wealthy people often took dinner (never served before ten) and afterwards danced until the wee small hours of the morning.

Shortly, my family and myself were to begin the long return trip, while the others left us at Hendaye on their way to see the two extraordinary caves of Tuc d'Audoubert and Les Trois Frères on Count Bégouën's estate in Ariège. Our party hired a car to take us back to Les Eyzies where I was to paint several more pictures before we returned to Paris. From time to time we heard from our friends who had gone to Southern France on their special mission and when that was accomplished they too returned to Paris to prepare for further visits to places on our way to the big Anthropological Congress held that year in Amsterdam. In the interval of several weeks while resting a bit, I painted a small full-length figure of the Abbé standing in his khaki cave suit with his cane and acetylene lamp, and smiling at us from a grotto entrance as we had seen him do so often in the weeks just passed. While posing (and I cannot claim that the Abbé was anything but a very casual model) we talked of many things, and I was to get further insight into the mind of this extraordinary man.

On to Amsterdam by train through Cologne and along the picturesque curves of the Rhine on its northern course to the sea. Amsterdam, cool and expensive, but for a couple of weeks the center of interest for world anthropologists, gave us all a really royal welcome. The Prince Regent, husband of Queen Wilhelmina, entertained the assembled scientists with an elaborate dinner at the great Krasnapolsky Restaurant, where we ate and drank with gusto and listened to an address from the Regent himself as well as a number of celebrated men from the four corners of the globe — all gathered to discuss with each other the latest finds in the great history of ancient man. A special scientific treat was the trip to Haarlem to hear Professor Dubois[35] discuss his wonderful find in 1891 of the skull

---

[35] Eugène Dubois (1858–1940) and *Pithecanthropus erectus* (now called *Homo/H. erectus*) encountered only scorn when he first announced his discovery of the "missing link"

cap and femur of a most primitive man-like being which he had named *Pithecanthropus erectus* — formidable but meaning simply "erect ape man." At the end of his discourse he showed for the first time in public these priceless relics of a very ancient type of humanity, which had lived perhaps 300,000 years ago in the forest of Java, and which indicated furthermore a closer affinity with the great primates than had ever been realized by the savants of the day. It was an impressive sight, the interior of that small room in Haarlem filled to suffocation with world experts on the subject who now for the first time were looking at the actual bones of the extremely ancient fossil while they listened intently to Dubois' description of the primitive creature, and how and where it was discovered on the great tropical island. This was really a memorable occasion and one not to be forgotten because of its extreme significance to science in general. The meeting was not all technical, however, as we made trips to Marken, and visited the splendid collections of the Rijksmuseum, where the ever memorable canvas of Rembrandt's "Night Watch" still glowed and sparkled in a brilliant and wonderful manner.

There were a number of very prominent men in the field of anthropology who contributed most interesting papers on the subject during the course of the meeting: Sir Arthur Keith, Sir Grafton Elliot Smith[36], M. [Eugène] Pittard from Geneva, the Abbé, of course, Count Bégouën, and

---

between apes and modern humans. His hypothesis was confirmed in the 1930s with a similar find by G.H. von Koenigswald in Java and D. Black's discovery of "Peking Man" in China. Current thinking once again casts doubt as to whether *H. erectus* is in fact one of our direct ancestors, though. The latest theory suggests that we and *H. erectus* may have both branched off from an earlier common ancestor called *H. ergaster* about 1.6 million years ago, leaving open the possibility that we, *H. neanderthalensis*, and *H. erectus* all existed at the same time.

[36] On the topic of missing links, Keith and Smith were among the many notable scientists (and others, including Arthur Conan Doyle) caught up in the (in)famous Piltdown Man hoax. The story of the forgery (see, for example, *Unraveling Piltdown*, by John E. Walsh, NY: Random House, 1996) serves as an object lesson in how science is a very human

scores of others — all interesting, well informed and experts upon their particular subjects. We just sat back and drank it all in with satisfaction and much intellectual profit. At the end of the session, the great concourse of scientists gradually dissipated, each either going back to his own country or making special excursions to other points in England and the continent, where might be found items of value for future thought and study. We had covered a good bit of country since the day when we left Paris for Les Eyzies, but the memory of that trip will always remain a bright spot in a world darkened always by the shadow of impending trouble.

endeavor. Scientists can stumble when caught up in the enthusiasm of a new discovery, especially in a field where scarcity of data is the rule rather than the exception, but eventually right themselves through their work and improve our understanding of the natural world.

Here his autobiography ends, leaving another large gap in the record of Charles R. Knight's life, in this case for the period during which he focused his attention on depicting the dawn of humanity — once again with uncanny accuracy even in the light of current scientific thought. What of the years in between 1900 and 1927, and those after? Well, as his granddaughter Rhoda Knight Kalt says, "He got bored with writing, and put it aside to get back to painting."

Stephen Jay Gould once said, "I cannot think of a stronger influence ever wielded by a single man in such a broad domain of paleontology." Knight did so by producing hundreds of illustrations, murals, and paintings that shaped the vision of a century of artists, scientists, and the millions who still admire his work in museums, magazines, and books. He died April 15, 1953. His last words to his daughter Lucy were "Don't let anything happen to my drawings."

Charles R. Knight, 1951

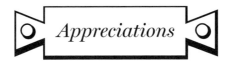

Appreciations

John Flynn

From leaping dinosaurs to crouching cats, Charles Knight was the first, and by many measures the finest, modernistic re-creator of ancient vertebrate life. By some marvelous stroke of luck, Knight has been with me throughout my life, from childhood visits to curatorships at the American Museum in New York and the Field Museum in Chicago. These museums are sites of some of his greatest commissioned works, which still instill wonder in millions of visitors, and inspire generations of scientists and natural history artists. In fact, his reconstruction of the crouching, snarling sabre-toothed cat *Smilodon*, a group of animals that I specialize in studying, remains one of the most vivid and vibrant natural history paintings ever created. Knight understood how animals lived and moved, arising from (and often in spite of) interactions with leading scientists, thorough study of anatomy and environments, and his own intense drive to create truly lifelike portraits of long-dead creatures. As a curator of fossil mammals, my old office desk sat beneath Knight's spectacular study painting of the "Irish elk" *Megaloceros*. I like to imagine that the sheer majesty of that giant extinct deer, with its powerful gaze reflecting Knight's watchful eye, spurred me to more imaginative thinking in my own work.

DR. JOHN FLYNN *is Frick Curator of Fossil Mammals and the incoming Chair of the Division of Paleontology at the American Museum of Natural History. A recent Guggenheim Fellowship winner, prior to joining the American Museum he was MacArthur Curator and Chair of Geology at Chicago's Field Museum.*

John Harris

Charles R. Knight was the first artist to portray extinct species as dynamic living entities and the sheer dynamism of some of his works still has the power to thrill today's audiences even though our knowledge of the anatomy and behavior of some of Knight's subjects, particularly the sauropod dinosaurs, has changed dramatically in the intervening years. Knight based his restorations of extinct creatures upon detailed studies of living animals and in so doing was able to impart vitality to creatures previously known only from dusty skeletons.

Knight's ability to make long extinct creatures come alive helped transform vertebrate paleontology from a hobby akin to philately to an interpretational science that added a temporal dimension to biology. His works inspired paleontologists to no longer be content with merely listing the physical differences between species but instead to investigate what such differences mean in terms of function and behavior, thereby increasing our understanding of the enormous complexity of the history of life on earth.

DR. JOHN HARRIS *is Chief Curator and Head of Vertebrate Studies at the George C. Page Natural History Museum of Los Angeles County. He was formerly the head of the Division of Paleontology at the National Museums of Kenya.*

Mark Norell

The early days of American fossil collecting generated immense public excitement as skeletons of huge animals with fearsome teeth and grotesque horns were assembled for display in the great museums like my own. These skeletons led to fantastic recreations of animals, drawings and paintings that portrayed these creatures as dragons, unicorns, and the stuff of bad dreams. But Charles Knight took the fantasy away. By combining his impressive anatomical and artistic skills and working closely with paleontologists and explorers he made these animals believable. By painting them into backgrounds, showing them dynamically interacting and behaving, he brought the past to life, and showed just how similar the present is to the prehistoric.

DR. MARK NORELL *is Chairman and Curator of the American Museum of Natural History's Division of Paleontology. His book* Unearthing the Dragon *describes the revolution in dinosaur paleontology caused by the discovery of China's feathered dinosaurs.*

Michael Novacek

Charles R. Knight, through his revolutionary renderings of the past, breathed life into fossils in drawers and skeletons on display. His depictions of these ancient worlds were not fabricated; they were based on solid scientific foundations. But the artist in Knight allowed him to infuse these reconstructions with a distinctive beauty and emotion.

When I was child I saw much of that ancient world through Charles Knight's eyes, images that still linger with me and countless others. Now at last, in this autobiography, we encounter vividly the childhood that formed the artist, the teachers who trained him, the scientists who influenced him, and of course the living world and ancient bones that inspired him.

DR. MICHAEL NOVACEK *is Provost of Science and Curator of Paleontology at the American Museum of Natural History, and author of* Time Traveler: In Search of Dinosaurs and Ancient Mammals from Montana to Mongolia *and* Dinosaurs of the Flaming Cliffs.

Ian Tattersall

Almost a century after Charles Knight began to produce life reconstructions of extinct human precursors and particularly of the Neanderthals, paleoanthropologists (whether consciously or otherwise) are still under the spell of these unparalleled evocations of our vanished precursors. Scientific understanding changes, but the perception, subtlety and dynamism of Knight's haunting images is undying, and makes them eternally relevant to the present.

DR. IAN TATTERSALL *is the Curator of the American Museum of Natural History's Division of Anthropology. His most recent books are* The Monkey in the Mirror: Essays on the Science of What Makes Us Human *and* The Last Neanderthal: The Rise, Success and Mysterious Extinction of Our Closest Human Relative.

Rhoda Knight Kalt

Toppy

In re-reading my grandfather's unfinished autobiography I can recall how often he spoke of what he wrote here. We would sit in the tiny kitchen of his apartment at 24 W. 59th Street in New York City — the apartment Toppy (my nickname for my grandfather) shared with my grandmother, Annie Hardcastle Knight, who I called Nonnie. They were a devoted couple and married for over fifty years. As I ate my breakfast in their tiny kitchen overlooking a pitch dark courtyard, Toppy would laugh and tell me stories — stories of his childhood, the Peck farm, the animals which he so loved, Lamb's studio, his work creating the animals for the stained glass windows, his first work at the American Museum of Natural History, his close friendship with Henry Fairfield Osborn, his trips to Spain with Henry Field, my mother, Lucy Hardcastle Knight, my grandmother and the Abbé Henri Breuil. He loved to tell how the Abbé instructed everyone to wash dirt off of the grapes in a glass of water — and then he drank the water!

Often Toppy polished his shoes or the silver spoons he kept in a jar on the table as he filled his granddaughter with wonderful stories and sang her songs. Toppy had a beautiful singing voice. His close friend Olive Fremstad (the great Wagnerian mezzo-soprano) wanted my grandfather to take singing lessons — begged him to take them! Toppy would laugh as he recalled this, and say "I told Olive that one Wagnerian singer was enough. And besides, she'd have wanted me to give all my time to singing lessons, and I had my art."

What was truly extraordinary was that my grandfather was born with very poor eyes. Near-sighted and astigmatic to begin with, later his cornea was severely scarred when he was struck in the eye by a stone as he played with children in his neighborhood. And much later in life he had both cataracts and a detached retina. I believe the latter caused his depression and ultimate heart attack and death, for Toppy's greatest fear was losing the little sight he had, and worked with, his entire life.

Each weekend and every summer of my childhood was spent with my grandparents. On the weekends I went with Toppy to the American Museum of Natural History, where we would roam the halls and speak with everyone! Toppy needed people — even when he painted he liked company and to talk. (His granddaughter is very much like him!) Toppy spoke to artists in the great halls of the Museum, making suggestions. They had no idea they were being trained by a renowned artist, but they would look stunned as he redirected their pencils and kept thanking him over and over. We'd lunch with the staff in a private dining room where I'd sit patiently as they discussed one fossil bone in endless detail. Then I'd climb the back stairs or take the old-fashioned elevator to the fifth floor, and there I met many of the great names of paleontology and anthropology: George Gaylord Simpson, Edwin H. Colbert, Harry L. Shapiro, James H. McGregor... And so it would go, often late into the night, when, the streets dark, we'd hail a taxi and return to my most patient grandmother. When Dr. Robert Broom, the renowned paleon-tologist, arrived in New York from the Transvaal Museum in Pretoria, South Africa I was allowed to sit between this great scientist and Toppy in a large limousine, as he accompanied Dr. Broom to the broadcast studio for an interview. Dr. Broom was then in his 80s, making his first trip to the United States. He later wrote me from Africa asking me to visit him with my grandfather. However my parents said five years was too young and kept me home. Was I angry!

Saturdays we went to the zoos and visited every sick animal to be sure they were getting the proper care. There was a yak at the Central Park Zoo who'd lost one of his horns, and was unable to raise his head, so he could only walk back and forth in his cage, head hanging to one side. I thought my grandfather would have to be taken to the hospital as he watched the yak in his suffering. (It made him even more sick to see the big cats caged and pacing back and forth. He would be so happy to see how things have improved.) Often as we stood beside a cage a crowd of fifty or more would gather around us as Toppy talked to me! And often four or five would be taken back to the studio for my grandmother's daily tea parties.

We also loved going to the Plaza Hotel for tea. I'd walk in my mother's high heels and my grandmother's chiffon stole, singing and dancing all the way to the steps of the Plaza. And then I'd feel so grown up sipping tea with Toppy and Nonnie in the Palm Court. Later we would walk down Fifth Avenue, stopping and looking in all the windows, especially the jewelry stores, discussing the depths of color and the facets. Occasionally Toppy went to the movies, and I recall how much he loved Sir Laurence Olivier in *Henry the Fifth*. We sat through the film twice so Toppy could watch Olivier, dressed in armor, ride through the army camp at night, the moon lighting his way.

The stories are endless, but so are the admirers of Charles R. Knight — wonderful artists and scientists of today who feel my grandfather has inspired their work. I would like to thank all of these artists, scientists, writers, and filmmakers for their love of Charles R. Knight. For in their love I have my grandfather with me forever. Through their love, my grandfather walks beside me. Thank you from my heart.

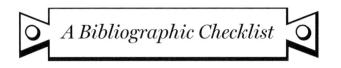

A Bibliographic Checklist

BOOKS

Czerkas, Sylvia M. and Glut, Donald F., *Dinosaurs, Mammoths and Cavemen: The Art of Charles R. Knight* (NY: E.P. Dutton, 1982).

Knight, Charles R., *Animal Drawing: Anatomy and Action for Artists* (NY: Dover, 1959, originally published in 1947 by McGraw Hill as *Animal Anatomy and Psychology for the Artist and Layman*).

_____, *Animals of the World for Young People* (NY: Frederick A. Stokes, 1908).

_____, *Before the Dawn of History* (NY: McGraw Hill, 1935).

_____, *Life Through the Ages* (Bloomington, IN: Indiana University Press, 2001, originally published in 1946 by Alfred A. Knopf).

_____, *Prehistoric Man: The Great Adventurer* (NY: Appleton-Century-Crofts, 1949, in which a differently edited version of his 1927 "Journey in Prehistory" appears).

Knight, Charles R. and Hardcastle, Ella, *Birds of the World for Young People* (NY: Frederick A. Stokes, 1909).

Stout, William, *Charles R. Knight Sketchbook*, Volumes I-III (Pasadena, CA: Terra Nova Press, 2002-2003).

ARTICLES

Anon., "Artist who makes the dry bones of science live," *Current Opinion*, vol. 73, November 1922, 646-647.

_____, "Charles R. Knight, Artist: An animal painter who looks backward on evolution," *World's Work*, vol. 49, March 1925, 498-504.

Czerkas, Sylvia Massey and Glut, Donald F. "Giving life to ancient bones," *Natural History*, v. 91, no. 2, February 1982, 57-61.

Dickerson, Mary Cynthia. "Charles R. Knight — Painter and sculptor of animals," *American Museum Journal*, vol. 14, no. 13, 1914, 83-98.

Gould, Stephen J, "Dinosaur deconstruction," *Discover*, vol. 14, no. 10, October 1993, 108-113.

Knight, Charles R., "Parade of life through the ages: Records in rocks reveal a strange procession of prehistoric creatures, from jellyfish to dinosaurs, giant sloths, saber-toothed tigers, and primitive man," *National Geographic Magazine*, vol. 81, no. 2, February 1942, 141-184.

_____, "Underseas forms of life," *Natural History*, vol. 20, no. 3, May-June 1920, 286-293.

_____, "What are they thinking?," *Natural History*, vol. 41, no. 2, February 1938, 85-89; 148-151.

Paul, Gregory S., "The art of Charles R. Knight," *Scientific American*, vol. 274, no. 16, June 1996, 86-93.

Peck, Robert M., "Forgotten cats of Charles Knight," *International Wildlife*, vol. 21, no. 5, September-October 1991, 18-23.

_____, "The artist who saw through time: Science illustrator Charles R. Knight (1874-1953)," *Natural History*, vol. 101, no. 8, August 1992, 60-63.

Wiley, J. P. J. "Dinosaurs shake the ground in paint and sculpture," *Smithsonian*, vol. 18, no. 3, June 1987, 84-89.